Merry Christmas
Darling
Dec 1975

Love and Best
wishes

Diana

Love Signs
PISCES

BY
DEREK & JULIA
PARKER

MITCHELL BEAZLEY PUBLISHERS LIMITED
London

Contents

© Mitchell Beazley Publishers Limited 1973

Edited and designed by Mitchell Beazley Publishers Limited, 14-15 Manette St., London W1V 5LB

Love Signs features work by the following artists: Ann Meisel, Diane Tippell, Elizabeth Klein, Michael Embden. Designer: Nick Eddison.

Derek and Julia Parker's new researches published in this book accompany original material by them, published in other works, which has been re-edited for *Love Signs*.

ISBN 0 85533 031 7

Printed and bound in the Netherlands

There's no doubt about it, Pisceans always have marvellously liquid eyes that even when full of happiness are also full of tears. When Pisces is in love, that love seems to filter through every expressive glance. When Pisceans fall in love they fall good and hard – they have a very high emotional level, and it is extremely important for them to channel this positively. Expression comes through any form of artistic activity. from poetry to dancing; but it *must* be there. If it is not, Pisceans can go to pieces and, like the fishes of their Sign, find themselves swimming in opposite directions, living with their conflicts and in extreme circumstances taking a negative, escapist way out.

Of course, artistic creativity apart,

The best way for Pisces to be at one with themselves is to have a satisfying emotional relationship; if their partner provides a strong arm to lean on, so much the better. Pisces is all aspiration, love and romance, so the partner must try to be the mould into which Pisces can pour all this, giving life a shape and meaning. For sometimes it is 'shape' and 'direction' in life that is lacking in the Piscean make-up.

Pisceans make marvellous lovers: they have so much to give, and will express themselves with great physical affection. They can send wonderful poems or love-letters – muddled and confused at time, perhaps, but quite unsurpassed in feeling and sentiment.

The position of the love planet Venus is very important when it comes to the Piscean love-life, and if it falls in Pisces with the Sun (see page 44), here is romance at its purest, with the highest possible emotional content – a rich, but gentle emotion. If Venus is in the glamourous Sign of Aquarius, the Piscean will have a slightly more detached view of love and sex, and could at times be cooler than an admirer might expect. If Venus is in passionate Aries, then there will be a much greater accent on passion, and the Piscean heart will burn a great deal more strongly than if, for instance, Venus is in Capricorn – on the chilly side for Venus!

Pisceans may well become confused when a loved one is around, and make unnecessary apologies for slight clumsiness. They should look out for this tendency, which can be irritating. They underestimate their charms and should try to relax a little more.

A date with a Piscean will be interesting and probably 'different'. One might be taken to a poetry reading (sitting on huge floor cushions in a rather way-out environment) or to a theatre-in-the-round or an art film. If a day out is planned, then it will be a quiet day on the river or the lakes, perhaps punting in some delightful backwater under willow trees . . . By the way, don't turn up before the appointed time – especially if you're calling for a Piscean. They won't be ready, and may answer the door in undress and confusion!

You and Aries

It will be a tremendously interesting experience for Pisces and Aries when they become friends. If they think about each other's characteristics, they can learn a lot. Pisces will be ready to admire the uncomplicated Arian attitude to life and its problems, while Aries will recognize the natural kindness, sympathy and charity of Pisces. But Pisces will find it difficult to accept Aries' tendency to selfishness. There is often a lot of intellectual *rapport* between these types. Aries is a strong positive, enthusiastic type and should be very good at giving tender and sometimes disorganized Pisces a little confidence. So Pisces should listen when Aries enthuses about some Piscean creative effort, and not be frightened or apprehensive about responding. Aries often likes sports – usually the tougher sports that don't always appeal to Pisces.

A Piscean man attracted to an Arian girl must remember that she is probably highly sexed, usually enjoys life in a bright and breezy sort of way, and may well not take her love life too seriously. There's no need for Pisces to beat about the bush or be at all shy; Aries likes directness and hates anything complicated or slow. He must remember that he will probably have rivals, but he could discover that he has a lot of emotional *rapport* with her. It's possible that Venus was in Pisces when she was born. If he can find out the exact date of her birth, this may reveal much (see page 44). Mars is her ruling planet, and will show how sexy she is.

When a Pisces girl is attracted to an

Presents that are sure to please

Arian man, she should put on a show of strength and independence in her approach. He likes girls who stand on their own feet, and will be

delighted if she comes straight to the point and suggests a lunchtime drin If he is attracted to her, she must expect the affair to develop quickly, for he's a fast worker. If she finds ou what Sign Venus (and more especial Mars) was in when he was born, this will help her to assess him (see pages 44 and 45). This may not be an easy affair, but there will be terrific moments and both should get a lot c fun and interest out of each other's company.

The emotional level of a marriage between Pisces and Aries will be extremely high, and both must realize that their individual characte are different. Pisces could easily mel into a pool of tears when Aries catches fire, flaring up almost without warning. But when Pisces is uncertain or worried, the Arian enthusiasm for life will be a great source of inspiration. This is not the easiest of combinations, but with mutual understanding it should become a truly rewarding marriage.

You and Taurus

The Taurean pace of life is slow, steady and usually calm, and Taureans are on the whole conventional. All these qualities are marvellous for Pisces, who is often not too well organized and tends to flap and flounder when he or she has problems. So when these types are friends, Pisces will find that Taurus is always there in the hour of need, ready to give support. Pisces will find Taurus to be tremendously practical – *not* a Piscean quality. And from Pisces, Taurus can learn to be less stodgy, less materially-minded. Pisces may also help Taurus to reassess his

or her opinions from time to time, as they can tend to get too set as Taurus grows older. Taurus appreciates beautiful things and will love visiting museums and art galleries with Pisces.

If a Piscean man finds a beautiful (but slightly overweight?) Taurean girl and simply offers her a good dinner, he will probably find that the battle is as good as won. She adores good food – but may have expensive tastes, so he should be prepared to spend a little more than he bargained for. He will find her passionate, but perhaps a little slow to arouse. This may just be because there's a conventional streak in her with which she has to battle. All Taureans are possessive, and while he may only be thinking of the affair in terms of 'fun', *she* may be more serious. If he finds out when she was born, he could discover (see page 44) that Venus was either close to his Sun or in her Sun Sign, which would give a touch of real romance.

When a Pisces girl finds a handsome,

dark-haired Taurean man, she shouldn't find it too difficult to catch his deep-set eyes. He will probably have good business sense, and, as hers is probably non-existent, she could ask his advice on anything from car insurance to what to do with an unexpectedly generous birthday cheque from Granny. He'll be romantic and not 'difficult' at all, so there shouldn't be complications. But like the girls of the Sign, he'll be possessive, and she should remember that.

Presents that are sure to please

When Pisces and Taurus marry, it'll be well for Taurus to do the budgeting and household accounts! Taurus will admire and appreciate the Piscean artistic flair, and the home (which may not be as tidy as Taurus would really like) will certainly be attractive and very comfortable. Pisces can help Taurus to be less purely materialistic, and the stability Pisces receives from the Taurean commonsense attitude to life is marvellous. The marriage should work out very well indeed, with each partner contributing something worthwhile to genuine and lasting companionship.

You and Gemini

One thing is certain: friendship between Pisces and Gemini won't be either soothing or relaxing! Pisces will discover that Gemini is never still, always doing more than one thing at a time. But Pisces, too, enjoys doing more than one thing at a time, and when these two Signs get together things can get out of hand. It's essential for both to make a great effort to *finish* projects they begin, and not to be too keen to get on with the next bright idea. Of the two, Pisces will find it easier to sit still and really *listen* to the record on the turntable, so he or she should try to make Gemini do the same, instead of looking through the pile to find the next one to put on, and secretly wishing there were another turntable in the room so that two records could go on at once . . . not to mention watching the picture on TV at the same time! If Pisces and Gemini can learn to *relax* in each other's company, they should enjoy life. Conversation will flow freely, and they will enjoy pouring out to each other their theories, ideas and innermost feelings – with Gemini, the logical and unemotional one, questioning and re-questioning them.

When a Pisces man meets a lively, flirtatious Gemini girl he'll soon realize that her duality affects her love-life in no small way. She'll probably have a whole string of lovers, and not take any of them too seriously. She's far less emotional than he, which might cause strain at times; but she's a challenge to the romantic, poetic Piscean. She likes variety and change of style in love-making – and, indeed, in partners. The affair will be 'different' and fun!

When a Pisces girl is attracted to a Gemini, she can easily attract his attention by asking him if he has a book that she's finding it difficult to get hold of. Once he sees she has plenty of lively and different interests, she'll not find it difficult to get acquainted – possibly over coffee, discussing the ailments of her pet fish or terrapin! She must remember that he'll be flirtatious, and probably

Presents that are sure to please

far less emotional than she; though she'll find him more sympathetic and emotional if Venus was in Cancer when he was born (see page 44). An interesting, lively relationship which could become a little edgy and restless at times, with not enough pure relaxation.

When Pisces marries Gemini, they may change homes rather more often than couples usually do: both partners should try consciously to overcome this inherent restlessness. Gemini must try to accept Piscean illogicality, and Pisces must try to recognize and control emotional tension. Both should be careful not to miss out on each other's good qualities.

You and Cancer

Though both Pisces and Cancer belong to the same 'element' (both are water Signs) and this develops sympathy between them, it does seem that very often friendship between them lacks a lively *rapport*. One tends to merge with the other, and to some extent there is a loss of individuality and identity. For instance, one may copy too closely the other's taste in clothes, which isn't a particularly good thing. Pisces must remember that Cancer, though kind and helpful, is sensitive and easily hurt. In fact, the emotional level of both is very high, and should they take themselves off to the cinema they could well flood the place with tears, because it's certain that the kind of film they will like will be a 'weepy'! But better to weep over a sad story than to give undue emotional content to some real situation, because of their fertile imaginations. Pisces and Cancer can get a lot out of life together by using their imaginations creatively – by writing children's stories, maybe, or by helping people in need.

When a Pisces man finds a romantic Cancerian girl (no doubt dressed in moonlight grey and with a pale complexion), he will discover that she is romantic but changeable: what is bliss at one moment may be

Presents that are sure to please

distasteful at another. Because Pisces is very flexible and may not want to be settled into a serious relationship, it could be necessary for him to remember that she will tend to be clinging and it may be difficult to end the affair when *he* wants to. Cancerians are often keen to have their own home and family, and in most relationships she forms a Cancerian girl tends to look at the man as a potential husband.

When a Pisces girl is attracted to a Cancerian man she will soon discover that he will want to protect and look after her. To what degree this is welcome is a matter for her. It could be marvellously welcome, in which case the search for the man in her life is probably over. He'll be both romantic and sensual, and he'll love *cooking*. She can easily attract his attention in the first place by asking him round for dinner – with a couple of other friends, for he might be shy on his own. (A delicious fish dish will make matters double sure!). A lovely, romantic affair: he'll be changeable

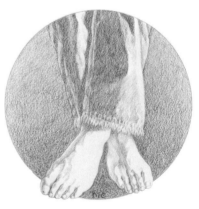

and moody, but she'll learn to cope.

When Pisces and Cancer marry they must seek some positive way – apart from sex – to channel their high emotions. Tensions could build up at times, but basically there will be considerable harmony. This combination makes for good parents. Pisces will find that Cancer is kind with children, but can be strict too – which Pisces *can't* be. This will need sorting out, because Pisces can tend to spoil the kids.

7

You and Leo

Many astrologers have the idea that 'water' and 'fire' Signs don't mix and throw up their hands at the thought of Pisces and Leo getting together. We couldn't agree less! This is a marvellous combination of types. Different though they are in many ways, there is plenty of common ground they can explore. Both have the reputation of being creative, and both are emotional – in exactly opposite ways. (The Piscean emotion, related to water, is illogical, flowing, deep; the Leonine, enthusiastic and passionate, like fire). So when the two become friends, a lot can happen; they won't find it in the least difficult to find joint interests. From classical ballet (many dancers belong to one of these two Signs) and the theatre (the same applies) to painting, designing, making clothes and unusual jewellery, poetry, photography and any other interest that helps to improve the quality of life and make it more beautiful . . . all are quintessentially Leonine and Piscean. Pisces will ease Leo out of pomposity; Leo, with enthusiasm and encouragement, will help Pisces to more sustained effort. An excellent combination!

When a Pisces man finds a blonde Leo girl he'll win his way into her heart if he pulls out all the romantic stops – perhaps even writing her

Presents that are sure to please

It's the full Cinderella bit when a Pisces girl finds herself a Leo Prince Charming. True to the fairy story, she'll just have to be around for a while for him (with a little encouragement) to sweep her off her feet. She must remember that he may be more conventional than her, and to gain more insight into his personality she should find out what Sign Venus and Mars were in when he was born (see pages 44 and

poems. He'll soon know whether she approves or not – and she very likely will, for it's easy for a Leo girl to be attracted to a Piscean man. Leo likes the best, remember, and hates anything done on the cheap. Pisces won't need to spend a fortune, but must make an effort: a well-packed picnic lunch will go down better than a cheap meal badly served in a café. For Leo girls, life must be pleasant, sunny, comfortable and elegant – – and it isn't *all* that hard for Pisces to fall in with the idea.

45). It shouldn't be difficult to discover a mutual interest – she could suggest a visit to an art exhibition. She will like his enthusiasm for life, and he will make her feel like a princess when they become lovers – helping her to greater self-confidence.

When Pisces and Leo marry, it's up to Pisces to realize that there is a domineering streak in most Leos. Pisces should not be afraid to point it out. The pair will be wonderful parents.

You and Virgo

Pisces and Virgo are opposites across the Zodiac, and, while they have many opposing characteristics, there is a natural *rapport* between them – a Piscean will always be able to see what a Virgoan is 'getting at', and vice-versa, whether they actually agree or not. Astrologers use the word *polarity* to describe these interesting indications.

Pisces will have plenty of time to drift off, dream and relax into a marvellously nebulous fantasy world when he or she has a Virgoan friend, for Virgo is a worker and will get the shopping, do the tidying, cook the lunch and be just as happy as Pisces. To Pisces (and any other type, for that matter) Virgo is a real helpmate, and loves it that way. However difficult it may be, it is very much up to Pisces to get Virgo to relax a bit, for it is good for Virgoans to be made to stop and enjoy some quiet, relaxing moments. Besides, Virgo's busy-busy habits can make Pisces a little nervous and restless which could be rather distressing. The two will soon develop hobbies. Virgoans are often good at such crafts as weaving and pottery – not without interest to Pisces. Virgo loves the country, too, and joint outings and days by the river are an excellent idea.

When a Pisces man is attracted to a modest Virgo girl he must remember that, no matter how romantic he may feel, he should take his time and approach her in a friendly way. Indeed, he may well be advised to keep the relationship on a 'friendly' basis for rather longer than he might with other types, as Virgo doesn't have a very high emotional level and it is sometimes difficult for her to come to terms with her love-life.

She's a bit clinical and rather critical of men, as well as being genuinely shy at times. If he helps her to 'settle' into the relationship, they could have a marvellous time; but it isn't always easy for her to be really affectionate or passionate. The positions of Venus and Mars when she was born (see pages 44 and 45) will have a powerful bearing on this area of her life. If Venus was in Virgo, she is likely to be *very* critical; if in Leo or Libra, then she should find it easier to enjoy her love-life.

A Piscean girl attracted to a neat, slick Virgoan male will not find it difficult to attract his attention if she asks him to do some small service

for her. To repay him, she might like to ask him to meet her friends, or give him some vegetarian food – so many Virgos are vegetarians. They will admire each other's contrasting qualities, and there will be sympathy between them.

When Pisces and Virgo marry there is a combination of inspiration, imagination, creativity, common-sense and practicality – the polarity of the Signs working at its best. Pisces will help Virgo relax, and must try not to 'catch' worry from him or her.

Presents that are sure to please

You and Libra

Will anything ever get done? Will the food be ready on time? Will there be a final decision about the holiday . . .? All are questions that spring to mind when one thinks of a friendship between Pisces and Libra. These are the most easy-going Signs, and while between them they will not lack inspiration and imagination, it won't be easy for them to come to definite decisions or to get themselves organized. They will certainly enjoy each other's company, and Pisces will respond well to the light intellectualism of Libra. Both like to enjoy life, but when they get together their joint characteristics will not result in a giddy social round but in quiet, gossipy evenings over a casual meal. The men of the Signs will probably enjoy a bit of fishing, and the girls will like days by the sea, or sewing sessions in winter. Music and poetry seem to be their art forms, and games such as tennis (when they feel energetic enough) are excellent for them. Pisces can find Libra rather resentful at times, and should try to help him or her see that this spoils their real, friendly personality.

When a Pisces man finds an attractive and pretty Libran girl, he'll only have to throw her the proverbial glance across the room and she'll come right over. He must remember that she's a tremendous romantic, but she could keep him waiting for an answer: Librans are notorious for shelving decisions. Atmosphere is important to both Signs, and it's often the case that they like similar settings, though Libra may want to go for rather more opulence than Pisces really cares for. Once Libra has made up her mind to accept him, the affair will be marvellous: very romantic, idealistic

Presents that are sure to please

and more than a bit out of this world

When a Pisces girl falls head over heels for a lovely, languid Libran, she should try at once to find out his taste in music, beg borrow or steal a few discs she knows will appeal to him, put on her most romantic Piscean dress, and give a party in his honour. She won't find him difficult to get to know, but she must expect a few rivals. She will do well to find out where Venus was when he was born (see page 44). He'll be the full Rudolph Valentino type if it was in Libra, with the Sun; if in Virgo, he may not have had an easy time with his love-life; if in Leo, he'll be the archetypal Big Spender!

When Pisces and Libra marry it won't be easy for either of them to get down to the business of running a home and raising a family. Both have plenty of love and affection to give each other and children, but such everyday things as organizing shopping-lists and making sure the kids get to school on time will have to be consciously sorted out.

You and Scorpio

If Pisces is a lovely, quiet, deep pool then Scorpio is a rushing surging torrent, and when the waters meet they blend and become one! Here we have the full emotional force of two water Signs coming together, and the first thing Pisces will realize about Scorpio is that he or she is strong and will provide a firm arm to lean on. Both have a very high emotional level, and they will sympathize with each other and share mutual respect. Scorpio is a great believer in getting at the truth, and will burn up a lot of energy to that end; Pisces is a humanitarian. If these two forces can be joined, the couple will between them do a great deal for the community – sorting out social injustices and giving help where it is most needed. Pisces will not care for Scorpio's jealous tendencies and will recognize a slight leaning towards cruelty at times, but can do a great deal to help Scorpio overcome this. On a 'fun' level, Scorpio likes to enjoy life, to work and play hard, and Pisces, being adaptable, will fall in line. As far as work is concerned, maybe Scorpio can help Pisces to be a bit better organized, so that energy isn't wasted.

When a Pisces male finds a sexy Scorpio girl, clad for certain either in leather or in a costume straight out of *Carmen*, he'll soon discover that she is very highly sexed and passionate. She should respond very well to him, and he shouldn't have a difficult time pursuing her. She will probably be pretty experienced even if young, and once they become lovers emotion will certainly run high. It will be an affair that neither of them will be likely to forget, with some exotic and erotic moments. Of course, it may be too highpowered to last. But if it does become permanent, they must expect to live their lives at a very high pitch indeed.

she may have to watch her weight. The affair will probably exhaust her, but certainly it will broaden her experience of men. She might do well to discover where Mars was when he was born (see page 45). Mars rules Scorpio, and will have a powerful effect on him.

Few dull moments in a Pisces/Scorpio marriage! Quite a few storms, in fact – but lots of fun too, and every bit of experience squeezed out of life. The worst Scorpion fault is jealousy, which is bound to be shown at times.

Presents that are sure to please

When a Pisces girl finds her Scorpio supreme, she should think carefully before committing herself: does she really want a sexually demanding relationship? If so, just a little more of her favourite perfume than usual, and her most daring dress, and he'll soon notice her! She'll have a good time and some expensive meals, so

You and Sagittarius

There is an interesting relationship between Pisces and Sagittarius, concerning Jupiter. That planet used to rule Pisces, just as it rules Sagittarius. But in 1846 Neptune was discovered, and gradually it has been recognized that that planet in fact rules Pisces. However, there remains a pleasant affinity between Pisces and Sagittarius, and it is often expressed by a harmony and sympathy between people of the Signs. Pisces will genuinely admire the warmth of the Sagittarian personality, and the natural ability to pass on enthusiasm and warm emotion – which indeed will help Pisces in many ways. Both Signs have high ideals and often a spiritual motivation for thought and action, expressed towards humanity in general. Sagittarius can often help Pisces should the latter slip into any form of negative escapism, for Sagittarius is the stronger of the two, and often tremendously philosophical. In mythology, the god Jupiter was full of fun – and when Pisces and Sagittarius become friends they will certainly have fun in each other's company. They will feel 'right' together, and in more serious moods will discuss everything under the sun – especially religion. Both Signs have a reputation for religious feeling, and Sagittarius will either accept an orthodox faith wholeheartedly or reject it equally strongly; Pisces

Presents that are sure to please

A Piscean girl will first of all notice the casual image of the Sagittarian male she admires; but then she must decide whether he's the sporty or the studious type. Sporty types can get a little too boisterous at times; studious types aren't so glued to their books that they exclude themselves from a lively sex life. She might consider taking up riding to share some of

could be attracted to the religions of the East.

When a Piscean man finds an attractive Sagittarian girl, he'll probably have few rivals for she will like to feel free and unclaustrophobic in emotional relationships. He mustn't expect to keep her to himself, though, for the same reason. She will have great enthusiasm for life and sex, and a generally optimistic outlook on life. A happy affair for him, with sex, friendship and intellectual *rapport*.

Sporty's fun: he'll surely be a good horseman. Sagittarians are usually uncomplicated and like a direct approach, so she needn't be shy about asking him round for coffee or drinks. If she (or a friend) plays Spanish guitar, that'll send him for sure and they'll be away on a delightful, fun affair.

The easy-going characteristics of Pisces and Sagittarius will help them develop give and take in marriage. The home could be chaotic, for neither Sign is renowned for tidiness.

You and Capricorn

Capricornians have such practical, steady, firm personalities that a Piscean can gain a lot from having a Capricorn friend. But the two differ so fundamentally that it would be impossible to list the differences between them. On the credit side, Capricorn will help Pisces steady him or herself during times of emotional stress, coming up with nice sensible, practical suggestions. But because Capricornians tend to become gloomy from time to time, it'll be very easy indeed for sensitive Pisces to catch the mood and for depression to reign supreme. But Capricorn isn't all hard work and gloom. It's surprising just how well he or she can trip the light fantastic when in a lively mood, and Pisces won't have to wait too long for that off-beat sense of humour to make its presence felt. A tricky but potentially a good combination of Signs, provided Pisces doesn't allow himself to be dragged into the doldrums when Capricorn's burdens become too heavy to hold.

A Pisces man and a chic, smart, prosperous Capricorn girl will probably find common ground in music. Discovering her taste, he could ask her to a recital or a concert, or just ask her home with friends to listen to records. He must remember that she may not be very emotional, but the way to her sometimes ever-so-slightly-wintry heart could be through music. She'll be an avid reader, too, probably liking great works of literature such as *War and Peace* – nothing flippant or too light. She's sometimes a social climber, liking to be impressed. She'll enjoy the country, especially mountain districts. She may well help Pisces psychologically (perhaps more than he may realize).

A Capricorn man could well be far more conventional than a Piscean girl, so she mustn't be too 'forward' in her approach: he could find that unfeminine! She will just have to exercise quiet charm – no casual suggestion for a quiet drink after the

Presents that are sure to please

office, that wouldn't do at all. But she could, after a while, lay on a small dinner party with him and a few of her less trendy friends. She could find him a bit unemotional and cool, but she if anyone, can warm him up. Pisces could get a real feeling of security, and Capricorn a good deal of colour, from the affair – so it's not all snobbery and icicles.

When Pisces and Capricorn marry, things should work out very well indeed. Capricorn can supply all the practical commonsense that's necessary to make the down-to-earth, house-running side of the marriage work, and Pisces can feel free to let his or her imagination run wild in decorating the house and providing a truly inspired and interesting background to the children's lives.

You and Aquarius

It's essential from the start of a friendship between Pisces and Aquarius that they realize that there are great temperamental differences between them. Pisces will soon discover that Aquarius is all logic – very cool and unemotional – while he or she is just the opposite. The friendship will be interesting for each of them and valuable for society, for they are both humanitarians, charitable, prepared to do anything for anyone. It may be that while Pisces actually goes to the sick and cares for them, Aquarius will get on with transporting blankets, clothes and vaccine to where they are most needed. Pisces will discover that Aquarian friends will love the theatre, films and many other art forms. They will appear to be extremely unconventional and way-out in their opinions, but can also be set in them (challenging them to be more flexible will be interesting for Pisces). Aquarius is very independent and can be a terrific loner, though friendly. Any life-style, once set, will not easily be changed. An interesting,

Presents that are sure to please

different, stimulating relationship for both.

When a nice, gentle, Piscean man finds a Snow Queen Aquarian, it will be as well for him to develop *friendship* first, for their attitudes to their love-life will be very different. He must try not to force emotional involvement on her too soon. She may well prefer ties of friendship to a passionate love affair because she has a fairly low emotional level and is also extremely independent. Even when sexually involved with men, she may not be really moved. Pisces may find this a little difficult to take, so the affair could be slow to start and may

suffer from a certain sense of detachment.

The situation is somewhat similar when a Pisces girl meets an Aquarian man. One way she could attract him might be by talking about astrology. Some Signs of the Zodiac are more attracted to the subject than others, and Aquarius (with Pisces, Leo and Virgo) lead the field. Like as not, she won't find it too easy to calculate Birth Charts, but will be good at interpreting them; he'll be fantastic at the mathematics, and keep her in place when her intuition gets out of hand. She may find he's a bit distant in love (the positions of Mars and Venus when he was born will tell her much about him – see pages 44 and 45). She mustn't overwhelm him with emotion.

The rational meets the emotional, the logical meets the intuitive when Pisces and Aquarius marry. All that is clinical, friendly but detached and at the same time cosy, warm and comfortable will come together. Will there be clashes? Usually Aquarius and Pisces have enough quality to prevent them.

You and Pisces

Pisceans are so flexible and adaptable that it won't be at all difficult for them to fall in line with each other when they form a friendship. Because of their natural adaptability, it may well appear to both of them that they are as alike as two peas in a pod. But the emphasis is on the word 'appear', for unless they were born in the same town at precisely the same moment they *won't* be all that alike. However, we don't feel that a pair of Piscean friends will run into any difficulty in the matter of temperament, or seeing eye to eye. But, heavens – *how* chaos can break out in practical matters!

'Did you go to the laundrette this morning?' – 'No, I thought you were going.' 'Where's the fish mousse, I want to put it on the table.' – 'Oh, I forgot to make it.' Typical snatches of conversation when Pisces and Pisces share a flat. But it'll be an attractive pad (when the Sunday papers aren't scattered all over the floor), for the Piscean taste is individual and charming. Life should pass swimmingly for two Piscean friends. When there are storms, they will be weathered jointly, but to avoid most of them a really conscious effort must be made to develop practical commonsense as regards the essential, mundane things of life. While Pisceans *can* live in a state of chaos, it can also get on their nerves at times . . .

It's very easy when a Piscean man is attracted to a Piscean girl, for he has only to ask himself how he likes to be approached – and treat the girl in the same way. She will, of course, have as high an emotional level as he, but

the real interest will come when they discover what Signs Venus and Mars were in when they were born (see pages 44 and 45). Venus in Aquarius will cool them down; nice if Venus is in Pisces; more passionate if in Aries. Making decisions about outings won't be difficult provided they make quite certain who's going to book coach seats, get theatre tickets etc.

Much the same applies when a Pisces girl finds a Pisces man. She can be her own, sweet, natural, unaffected self – and when their eyes meet, they'll hear

the strings of the largest orchestra on either side of the Atlantic murmuring away. Whether they dance all night, make love or just sit in a corner reciting *The Wind in the Willows* to each other, they'll be all set for a delicious, emotional affair.

When Pisces and Pisces marry, the marriage should have a happy and carefree atmosphere. But Pisces can at times be plagued by emotional tension and worry, and when this happens to one partner it's important that the other doesn't get caught up in it too.

Presents that are sure to please

Making the most of Pisces

Piscean colours are the colours of the sea, in all its moods but especially when it takes on mysterious shades of green and blue. Neptune, the ruling planet of the Sign, certainly holds court in the Piscean kingdom, and its influence is felt not least in this delightful range of colours.

Pisceans are delightful, kind, unassuming, and certainly out of this world, from time to time! But they all too often tend to go in for the full Cinderella bit, and it really takes a Fairy Godmother gently but firmly to get them to make the most of themselves. They have great natural charm, and they don't have consciously to do anything about *that*, for it permeates their whole personality. But in spite of the fact that they can look terrific in rags or in the most expensive Paris creation, they do sometimes need to be persuaded to buy a new blouse, for example, or finish the hem on the dress they made last year and have worn quite a few times since, and *not* to cut the back of their hair themselves!

The girls of the Sign should stick to the lovely, soft clothes they look so good wearing. If they have to work in offices, or somewhere where colleagues dress in slick suits, they can probably get away with soft wool in winter, rayons and fine Indian cotton in warmer weather. In the evenings, they will almost certainly come up with something pretty unique, draping a sari or a length of delightful fabric round themselves or perhaps wearing some fantastic theatrical costume they found in a secondhand store down the road. If the Pisces girl is really going to make the most of herself, she should consider time factors, for all too often she has to rush at the last moment and spoil the overall effect as a result. The Piscean girl may well have to make a very conscious effort to buy accessories. There's no doubt about it, she likes and probably needs a large duffle-bag into which she can throw her ballet-shoes, leotard and tights – not to mention toilet-water and the weekend shopping as well.

Piscean girls either have dozens of pairs of marvellous shoes for their delightfully neat feet, or slop around in very old sandals until they fall to pieces and the shoe-shop has to be visited at last!

Many a Piscean likes to go barefoot, and while this is fine they must remember at the same time that because the feet are 'ruled' by Pisces, they are terribly vulnerable and could suffer more easily than Pisces may like to think from infections and other ailments.

The Piscean girl will look good in an assortment of long strings of glass beads in various pale colours matching her ensemble; perhaps she will collect some semi-antique ones, which will really do something for her. Her metal is tin, which doesn't respond too well to the jeweller, being so soft and easily damaged – though its softness makes it easily workable, and a good material for the amateur designer. Silver jewellery will suit her equally well, however. The bloodstone is the Piscean gem – interesting, secretive, mysterious, 'different', and therefore full of just those qualities to appeal to a Piscean.

The Pisces male can be almost as interestingly different in his attitude towards clothes as his female counterpart. He can look super in an old velvet jacket. In most Piscean males the real romantic, poetic image is crying to be let out, so why not let it? It may not be to everyone's taste to go around looking like something out of *Les Sylphides*, but a velvet suit over a soft shirt can look quite delightful.

Although, generally speaking, Pisceans do not have vast appetites, they have an above-average tendency to put on weight. Crash diets may not be easy for them, so something more gradual – giving up sugar in coffee? – might be a better idea.

Pisces' pad will have plenty of floor cushions to lie on. We might get a whiff of incense as we enter, and there will be arrangements of dried grasses and bullrushes, and perhaps a fishtank or two. This delicious atmosphere will set off the Piscean image to the full, helping them to get their loved one into *their* mood, so that the process of developing a romance will be made easier for them.

The real astrology

Astrology at work

'The celestial bodies are the cause of all that takes place in the sub-lunar world'–
THOMAS AQUINAS

For many centuries, from the earliest years of astrology, men believed that the planets' effect was supernatural – at first they were associated with the gods, and later it was still believed that their action was in some way spiritual. But modern astrologers look at it another way.

It is now more often believed that the positions of the planets at any one moment in time have an effect on earth through some force like, but not the same as, that of gravity. Science tells us that during the first half-hour after conception many human traits, physical and psychological, are formed within the tiny egg that is to become a man or woman. It may be at that time that the planets (known to affect vegetable and plant growth and the behaviour of animals) also affect the human egg and the subsequent life of the child – among other things, his or her human capacity for affection, friendship and love.

Scientists rather than astrologers must discover precisely 'how astrology works': at the moment we know nothing about the kind of force that can cross the vast reaches of space between Pluto and Earth and have an effect on human life. But compared with the unimaginable distances of outer space, the solar system is a small and compact unit, not unlike an atomic nucleus. In a sense, it would be extraordinary if the planets that nestle around the Sun did not affect us on Earth. As J. S. Haldane put it: 'The universe may be not only queerer than we suppose, but queerer than we *can* suppose!'

The solar system, with the Sun at its centre. Copernicus, in 1548, put forward the theory that the Sun, rather than Earth, was at the centre of the system. The general theory of astrology was not affected by this, as Isaac Newton who developed it, knew.

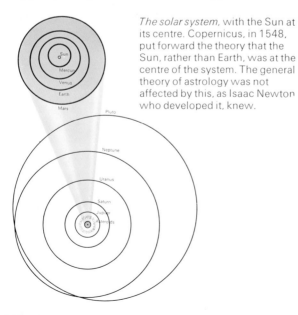

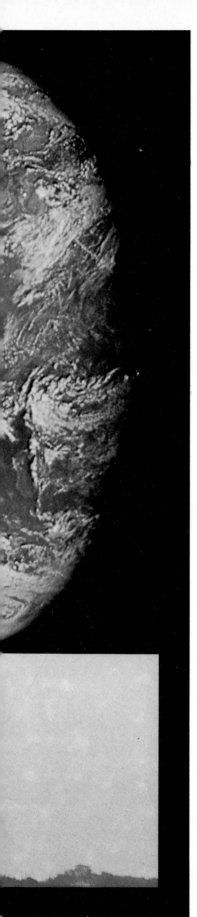

How astrology began

Out of the darkness of infinite space appeared visible signals of fate ; and man rejoiced' – ALFRAGANUS

Astrology must have started, in ages so remote from our own that all trace of them has vanished, by man noticing the simplest facts: that the Moon affected the tides, and made fishing easier or more difficult; that when Mars showed his red face in certain areas of the sky, a tribe fought more fiercely . . . Then, in clear Eastern skies, the seven planets known to ancient man were observed to make a pattern in the heavens – a pattern that meant something.

It was when a well-organised priesthood grew up in Babylonia that man really began to study the planets' effects on human life – at first very simply, noting only the moments when planets rose and set – but then observing too the effects of planets at certain angles to other planets. Written notes of planetary movements exist from 747 BC, so astrology has a *written* history of over 2,700 years.

Astrologers were engaged by kings and princes, and, by studying their Birth Charts, would predict wars or rebellions, plenty or famine. It was not until the 5th century BC that astrologers began using their science to help individual men and women plan their lives. The earliest personal horoscope that has been found is dated 409 BC, and in the following two centuries astrologers were writing much the same kind of reports for parents that astrologers write today. In 158 BC an Egyptian astrologer wrote to an expectant father: 'If your child is born when Jupiter has come forth,he will become rich,his days will be long . . .' Another Egyptian told a man 'born on the 5th Phaophi' that he would 'die of excessive love-making'!

By the time astrology had developed in Egypt, astrologers had agreed on the planetary influences. But the symbols of the Zodiac Signs – Taurus the Bull, Sagittarius the Archer, and the rest – were slower to emerge and their history is complicated. At various times there were many more than twelve constellations taken into account by Egyptian astrologers, including Pleiades (The Hair Brush)

and Auriga (The Sickle Sword).

From Babylonia and Egypt, astrology, with its increasingly complex history, spread to Greece – where Plato, Hippocrates and other philosophers advised its study – and then to Rome, where it became important at all levels of life – used by Emperor and Empress, and by the man and woman in the street, in politics and war, business and love. All the Roman emperors found a use for it. Some were able themselves to set up Birth Charts, others banished all astrologers from Rome except their own, so that no one planning a rebellion or an assassination would be able to make sure that the planets were on his side.

The first comprehensive astrological textbook came in the 2nd century AD – the *Tetrabiblos* of the great Greek astronomer Ptolemy, who collected together all previously-known data and set it out in a book which is still read today.

From Ptolemy's time until the beginning of the 19th century, astrology was of importance in every civilised country. Sometimes it was condemned, but more often it was taken for granted as a science too useful to neglect. The kings and queens of Europe ruled by its aid; ordinary people sought help in illness or in love – one English astrologer of the Elizabethan age, Simon Forman, left his papers to an Oxford library and in them can be read extensive notes of his help in other people's love affairs, and his own. John Dee, a brilliant scholar with the largest library in Europe,was astrologer to Elizabeth I of England; for some years she called on him every day for advice on home and foreign policy. Shakespeare's plays show how great a part astrology played in the everyday life of Elizabethan England. A century later, William Lilly advised both Charles I *and* Oliver Cromwell, but also gave advice to the love-lorn. Even during the years when astrology was under a cloud, lovers still 'asked the stars' when it would be best to kiss, to propose, to get married.

The birth chart

The complete Birth Chart is a map of the sky for the moment and from the place of birth

Below is a complete Birth Chart, used by an astrologer to discover the true potentialities of a client – his or her strong and weak points, the most suitable career and, of course, where he or she might expect to find most happiness in love. Earth is the centre of the Chart. Around it, the twelve equal Signs of the Zodiac form a band against which the planets move. The astrologer has placed them precisely as they were at the moment when his client was born. Everyone has *all* the planets and *all* the Signs in his or her Birth Chart. By looking at their positions – in relation to the Earth and to each other, in the twelve Signs, and in the 'houses' (the twelve inner segments of

the Chart) – the astrologer begins to interpret the effect they have on the client's personality. The Sign the Sun occupies (in this case, Gemini) is important; but so too is the Ascendant (Pisces), the Midheaven (Sagittarius), the Sign the Moon is in (Pisces), and all the rest.

To discover trends in their clients' future lives (astrologers never 'foretell the future'; the planets cannot dictate what *will* happen, they can only suggest what *may*), astrologers 'progress' the Birth Chart. Having calculated the precise position of every planet at the moment of birth, they use one of several methods to 'move' them to

new positions that symbolise possible future pleasures or hazards: when, for instance, you might expect a romance or even marriage.

The Signs and planets are represented by *glyphs* or symbols, some of which are ageless. The glyph for the Sun has been found carved on rocks from distant ages all over the world.

Each planet 'rules' a Sign, which means that it is stronger when placed in that Sign at birth. It also has a special relationship with other planets, according to the Signs they are in. Below, the planets (inner circle) are shown 'in' the Signs they traditionally rule.

Ascendant or Rising Sign
The sign rising on the eastern horizon at the moment of birth: here shown as 24° Pisces; once the position of the Ascendant is calculated, the other signs follow in order round the Chart.

Cusp of First House
The inner circle of the Chart is divided into 12 equal Houses; the First House occupies the 30° area below the eastern horizon; the cusp marks its starting-point.

Moon's Nodes
The nodes are the north and south points at which the Moon crosses the ecliptic: the north node is shown here in Pisces, the south node is at the opposite point in Virgo.

Glyphs of Planets
The glyphs of the planets (Saturn is the example marked here) are placed round the Chart and their exact positions at the moment of birth are noted in figures.

MC or Medium Coeli
The MC (Midheaven) is the point at the moment of birth when the ecliptic crosses the subject's meridian; in general terms the MC is the overhead point in the sky.

Glyphs of Signs
The sign glyphs, like that of Scorpio indicated here, are inserted round the Chart once the Ascendant is calculated. The glyphs are an extremely ancient form of shorthand.

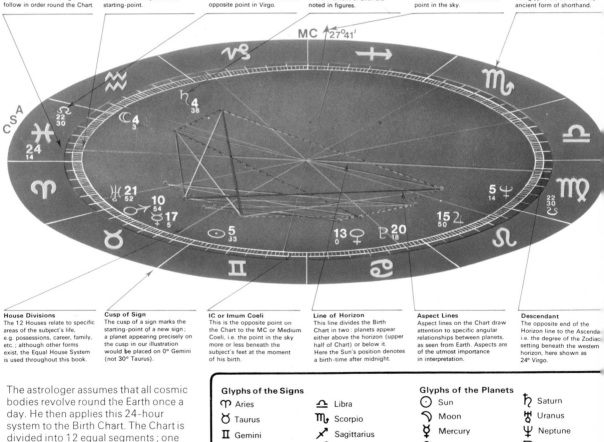

House Divisions
The 12 Houses relate to specific areas of the subject's life, e.g. possessions, career, family, etc.; although other forms exist, the Equal House System is used throughout this book.

Cusp of Sign
The cusp of a sign marks the starting-point of a new sign; a planet appearing precisely on the cusp in our illustration would be placed on 0° Gemini (not 30° Taurus).

IC or Imum Coeli
This is the opposite point on the Chart to the MC or Medium Coeli, i.e. the point in the sky more or less beneath the subject's feet at the moment of his birth.

Line of Horizon
This line divides the Birth Chart in two: planets appear either above the horizon (upper half of Chart) or below it. Here the Sun's position denotes a birth-time after midnight.

Aspect Lines
Aspect lines on the Chart draw attention to specific angular relationships between planets, as seen from Earth. Aspects are of the utmost importance in interpretation.

Descendant
The opposite end of the Horizon line to the Ascendant i.e. the degree of the Zodiac setting beneath the western horizon, here shown as 24° Virgo.

The astrologer assumes that all cosmic bodies revolve round the Earth once a day. He then applies this 24-hour system to the Birth Chart. The Chart is divided into 12 equal segments; one segment, or House, equals 2 hours. Outside the inner circle, the 12 equal Zodiac signs are plotted for the moment of birth.

Glyphs of the Signs		Glyphs of the Planets	
♈ Aries	♎ Libra	☉ Sun	♄ Saturn
♉ Taurus	♏ Scorpio	☽ Moon	♅ Uranus
♊ Gemini	♐ Sagittarius	☿ Mercury	♆ Neptune
♋ Cancer	♑ Capricorn	♀ Venus	♇ Pluto
♌ Leo	♒ Aquarius	♂ Mars	☊ Moon's Nodes North
♍ Virgo	♓ Pisces	♃ Jupiter	☋ South

Signs of the Zodiac
How the heavens determine character

hough astrological columns print paragraphs suggesting what the future has in store for 'Aries' or 'Gemini', this can be only very roughly true, for you – and what may happen to you in the future – are a mixture of all the influences of all the Signs, more or less stressed by the position of the planets within them. Though if you were born at or near sunrise, you may find that the news for 'Gemini', or the character-analysis of 'your' Sign printed in a magazine or newspaper, is more accurate than for other people. This is because the Sun Sign in your Birth Chart will be the same as the Ascendant (the Sign rising above the horizon at the time of your birth, and another important area of your chart). And if you were born at the time for a new Moon, as well as at sunrise, your Sun Sign will be even more emphasised, because the Moon, Sun and Ascendant will all be in the same Sign. But even then, the full Birth Chart should be calculated before you can really be sure that you know the whole truth about your astrological self.

Your Sun Sign – and you will certainly know what *that* is, because it depends on the time of year you were born; it is what people mean when they say 'I am a Leo' or 'an Aries' – generally shows the image you present to the world. The Ascendant, which you can only discover by having it calculated,

represents your inner, 'true' self. You may behave or look very like a Leo, but if your Ascendant is, say, Sagittarius, then your real inner self will be very different from your outward behaviour and appearance. So read Sun Sign descriptions for amusement; in this book, the position of Mars and Venus help to fill out the picture.

A professional astrologer will go much further, considering not only planetary positions but also the angles between the planets, the relevant 'polarities' – triplicities and quadruplicities. Polarities link the qualities of the Signs in an interesting and strong way. Aries people, for instance, may tend to be somewhat self-centred; Librans (Libra is the opposite Sign to Aries across the Zodiac) tend to be strongly geared to 'the other person'.

The Quadruplicities again group Signs of the Zodiac together and give them certain qualities. People with an emphasis on Cardinal Signs (Aries, Cancer, Libra, Capricorn) tend to be enterprising and outgoing. An emphasis on Fixed Signs (Taurus, Leo, Scorpio, Aquarius) prompts

resistance to change. Those with many planets in the Mutable Signs (Gemini, Virgo, Sagittarius, Pisces) tend to be adaptable and subject to change.

The qualities that the Quadruplicities show must be considered in relation to the Triplicities, and also, as always, to the appearance of the whole Birth Chart.

The Keywords are a shorthand way of remembering very roughly the qualities of each Zodiac Sign: they represent the way in which each Sign expresses itself. The keywords for Aries are 'assertively, urgently'. For Taurus: 'possessively, permanently'. Gemini: 'communicatively, adaptably'. Cancer: 'protectively, sensitively'. Leo: 'creatively, impressively, powerfully'. Virgo: 'critically, analytically'. Libra: 'harmoniously, together'. Scorpio: 'intensively, passionately'. Sagittarius: 'widely, freely, exploratively'. Capricorn: 'prudently, aspiringly, calculatedly'. Aquarius: 'independently, humanely'. Pisces: 'nebulously, impressionably'.

The Triplicities
Zodiac Signs are divided into Fire Signs, Earth Signs, Air Signs and Water Signs — astrologers find that when, for instance, Water Signs are emphasised by the planets in them at the time of birth, the subject has some of the qualities of the 'watery' Signs.

Fire Signs contribute enthusiasm

Earth Signs, stability and practicality

Air Signs, intellectualism, ease of communication

Water Signs, emotion and intuition.

Synastry
Charting the chances of love

This whole book is about what astrologers call 'synastry' – in its simplest form. When two clients ask an astrologer just how well they might get on in love or marriage, it won't be possible to tell them simply after discovering their Sun Signs. Even the positions of Mars and Venus in their Birth Charts won't decide the matter.

The astrologer will draw up both their Birth Charts, complete, showing all the planets in all the Signs, and the two Charts will be compared with great care before anything at all is said. And even then, the astrologer will be very careful indeed. What he or she will do is point out the areas of their lives in which they are likely to find agreement and happiness, and those other areas where there might be some difficulty.

Julia Parker, a consultant astrologer, has worked on many pairs of Charts on this basis, and has tried to do the same in this book. That is, she has tried to hint fairly strongly at the similarities and differences between the Sun Sign characteristics, and has sometimes suggested that the positions of Venus and Mars (pages 44-45) may be helpful. But of course it would be silly to drop a new friend because 'the stars' don't seem to be on the side of friendship. There may be other factors in the complete Birth Charts which promise well.

The serious astrologer uses synastry – the comparison of Birth Charts – in many ways: not only when marriage is a possibility, but when there is perhaps a prospect of a marriage breaking up. The astrologer will then compare not two but three Charts – those for Mr. A and Mrs. A and X, the other man or woman in the case. By 'progressing' the Charts, it is almost always possible to tell, for instance, if the extra-marital affair is one that is going to last or is just a passing infatuation.

Synastry can explore business partnerships or look at the parent/child relationship (see opposite). It can also be used in the teacher/

Tina and Tony were engaged. They knew their Sun signs – Tina was Taurus, Tony was Aries – and they were worried when they found a book that said, 'Aries and Taurus rarely get on together, and marriage would be unwise.' Unhappy, they went to consult an astrologer.

She was a reputable astrologer. 'That's nonsense,' she said, 'a huge over-simplification. What really matters is the story of your Birth Charts as a whole.'

She drew up complete Birth Charts for them both. 'Popular astrologers are *so* unreliable,' she said to herself. 'It's quite clear, from their Charts, that Tina and Tony will get on very well in marriage.'

Tina and Tony were thrilled when the astrologer told them. 'Naturally, there are certain areas where you can expect to disagree,' her report warned. 'But I have no doubt that, if you play down your differences, you will both be very happy. And, you know, they were.

student situation, and in many others. One thing is very important – in all aspects of astrology, but perhaps more so in synastry. That is that the full birth data must be available. Sometimes a boy will bring his own birth-date, time and place, but only the girl's birth-date. This means that astrologer will not be able to work out the all-important Ascendant, or

the Sign on the Midheaven (see page 20), and some factors will be missing from the assessment that can be made.

Critics have accused astrologers of trying to 'run people's lives'. But the destiny of friends and lovers is in their own hands. The planets can help or hinder – but can be overruled.

Helping children grow

'It is a wise father that knows his own child' — SHAKESPEARE

Professional astrologers spend a great deal of time working on the Birth Charts of children, for many parents realise that they can give real help with education, career problems, hobbies and, perhaps most important, the relationship between children and their parents.

Examining the Birth Chart of a newly-born baby, the astrologer cannot be of great help in suggesting what may happen to the child in the first ten years of its life, though it is often possible to suggest at what ages he or she may experience the normal illnesses of childhood. But it will certainly be possible to suggest the kind of toys the child will like the best, and, by comparing its Birth Chart with the Charts of both parents, to suggest how he or she will react to father and to mother in the years of childhood – from which parent criticism and discipline will be best accepted, and what form that discipline might most usefully take.

As the child grows up and starts school, it will be possible to tell the parents which subjects it might be profitable to concentrate on, which games the child will like, and what sort of school would be best – permissive or well-disciplined, single-sex or co-educational. And when the time comes to think about a possible career, the astrologer will be at his most helpful, advising a particular course before even the child is fully aware of what he or she wants to do.

Through the difficulties and joys of puppy-love to the first confusing experiences of sex and the first serious love affair . . . there is

practically no area of life in which an astrologer's advice cannot be helpful. Again, a look at the parents' Birth Charts will show which is best able to cope with the adolescent problems of a growing boy or girl, and many a generation gap has been narrowed considerably with the assistance of a good astrologer. No wonder many fathers now wait stopwatch in hand for the first cry. Of course, astrology alone does not account for how a child grows up: his surroundings, his ancestors also influence him. But looking at the Birth Charts of an entire family (*above*), the astrologer often sees an astrological pattern quite as strong as the genetic one. A prominent Sign will re-assert itself in a grandchild; a father's Ascending Sign will appear as his son's Sun Sign; in most families, five of the twelve Signs crop up again and again.

Another fascinating area of astrology is the 'astrological twin' – very

rarely, two babies will be born in the same hospital within one or two minutes of each other and will have virtually identical Birth Charts. Astrologers find this fascinating, for watching the development of these 'twins' it is possible to see clearly how events in their lives mirror each other, though of course under different circumstances.
Even 'identical twins' are not absolutely alike in every respect. Even if the births are only a few minutes apart, celestial traffic will inevitably have moved on during that time. So an astrologer looking at twins born, say four minutes apart, will be able to tell the parents which may have most will-power and determination, which may be inclined to worry or become tense. There will be small but sometimes important differences between their two Birth Charts – a planet may have changed Houses (see pages 46-47), or may have moved significantly to or away from an important angle in the Chart.

Planets of love

Astrology is astronomy brought to earth and applied to the affairs of men' — EMERSON

In this book we can deal only with the Sun Sign – the Zodiac Sign in which the Sun was placed at the moment of birth – and the positions of Venus and Mars (see the tables on pages 46-47). An astrologer advising anyone about their love-life, or perhaps the end of an affair, would rely on a full Birth Chart (see page 20). For of course it is not only the position of the Sun which has an effect on one's love-life, but *all* the planets in *all* the Signs.

THE SUN This book is largely based on the effect the Sun has on love when it is in various Signs. Pages 46-47 are based on this.

VENUS is associated with the desire for lasting partnership. It can make one over-gushing, over-romantic – but the positions of other planets will affect this. For the position of Venus in your own Chart, consult pages 44/46.

MARS If Venus is a feminine and romantic plant. Mars is masculine and sensual. It can make one rather selfish and hasty – but see pages 45/47 for its position in your Chart.

THE MOON can be responsible for emotional distrubances. It can make one patient and sympathetic – and also changeable and narrow-minded. It moves very quickly and its

position must be carefully calculated.

MERCURY affects communication with other people, affecting the way you talk to them and put over your feelings. It will either be in the same Sign as your Sun, or the one on either side. If you are Aries, for example, your Mercury will either be in Aries, Pisces or Taurus.

JUPITER In Holst's suite *The Planets*, Jupiter is called 'the Bringer of Jollity', and can indeed contribute generosity, enjoyment, sheer *fun* to a affair, particularly if you happen to meet a partner whose Jupiter is in the same Sun as your own. This planet stays in each Sign for a year.

SATURN That icy planet, Saturn, can really cool down an affair, for it can make one cautious, thrifty, selfish – break things up in no time at all!

URANUS can make one versatile and original, but it can also contribute eccentricity and even perversion. But at work in two Charts it can also mean a sudden dynamic attraction.

NEPTUNE Those with Neptune strong in their Chart will be idealistic, sensitive, spiritual – or could be deceitful, sentimental and indecisive, depending on the rest of the Birth Chart. But the planet can certainly bring romance! Those born

Take him and cut him out in little stars, And he will make the face of heaven so fir That all the world will be in love with night . . SHAKESPEARE

between 1915-1928/9 will have Neptune in Leo; between 1928/9-1942/3 in Virgo; between 1942/3-1956/7 in Libra. If Neptune is in Leo, it can contribute glamour and perhaps self-satisfaction; if in Virgo, an over-critical attitude; if in Libra unworldly idealism and perhaps an attraction to drugs.

PLUTO affects the beginnings or endings of affairs – the ability to make a new start perhaps under difficult conditions. From 1913/14-1937/8 Pluto was in Cancer; from 1937/8-1957 in Leo; from 1958/9-1971 in Virgo. Pluto in Cancer involved its generation in sudden changes in family life – often the disruption suffered during wartime. In Leo, Cancer seems to be prompting increased interest in mass social security and love for the whole family of nations and its environment. In Virgo, it could lead to a total re-evaluation of personal relationships, love and the family.

When reading forecasts in newspapers and magazines, do remember that the are over-simplified. The *planets*, as well as the Signs, are important!

Venus, as seen from Earth is very beautiful but its dense atmosphere would prevent anyone on it from seeing the Sun.

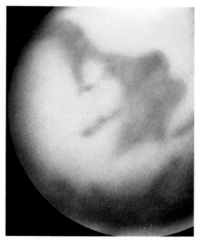

Mars is a much smaller planet than Earth, and there is now doubt about the existence of life on its surface.

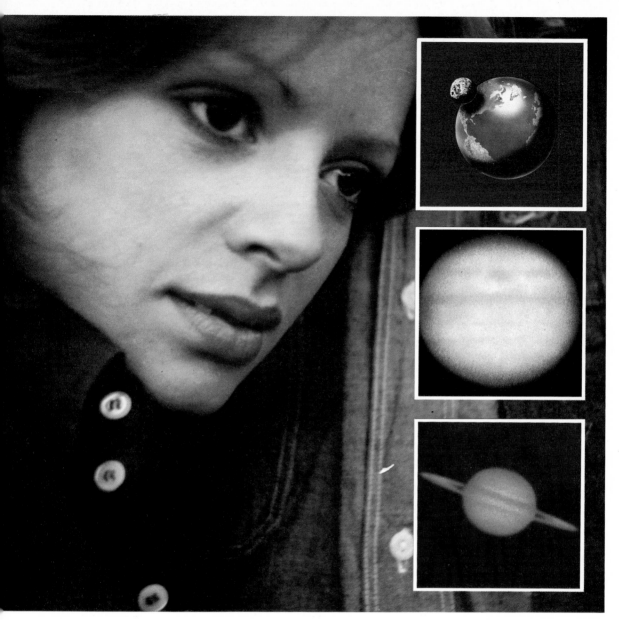

Astrologers throughout the ages have had to deal with the problems of love. How can they help? Certainly *not* simply by comparing one Sign with another and saying 'No, an Aries should never marry a Libra' or 'Yes, Gemini will always be ecstatically happy with Aquarius.' Ignore any astrologer or magazine-writer who says that kind of thing. For just as in every other area of life, what matters is not the Sun Sign alone but the whole Chart, and an astrologer asked whether Jack will be happy with Jill will compare the two Birth Charts (more about this on page 20), then point out where there would probably be happiness and where there might also be friction

But how do astrologers know when

romance is about to blossom for us? Modern astrologers do not predict events, but can discover periods when an emotional relationship may deepen, though not when one *will* get married. As one gets older, one's Birth Chart grows older too, and during the growing process the planets in the Chart make new relationships to each other, which themselves in time break up, more forming in their place. When, for instance, Venus and the Sun come together or Venus and romantic Neptune shake hands, there is a powerful emphasis on the love-life.

But do the planets then *compel* two people to love or not to love each other? Of course not. Even a couple with dreadfully clashing Charts

It is the stars, The stars above us, Govern our conditions' – SHAKESPEARE

The Moon (top), tiny compared to the Earth, is still the nearest planet to us, and can make a lover moody.

Jupiter (centre) and Saturn (bottom) are opposites: one brings jollity and fun, the other coolness and difficulty.

would have a chance together, for, as the old astrological motto says, 'The stars *incline*, they do not compel'. Man (and woman) is still master of his Fate. Certainly, when you are thinking of that first date, it can do no harm at all to find out where his Mars is, or where her Venus. But if you are attracted to each other – go ahead. The most the planets can ever say is, 'We told you so!' They will never claim that they made the match.

25

Astrology and the body

'A physician without knowledge of astrology has no right to call himself a physician' — HIPPOCRATES

Astrology has always been linked with medicine. In earlier centuries a doctor was almost invariably also an astrologer – in fact, one was not allowed to study medicine unless one also studied planetary effects on the human body, in sickness and health.

When a man or woman took to bed with an illness, the astrologer would immediately draw up a Chart showing the positions of the planets at the time. Since the various parts of the body were traditionally influenced by certain Signs, it would at once be possible to see where the illness was seated and just how serious it was. The treatment would follow accordingly. Perhaps herbs would be administered, often gathered at specific times to enable the planets to have their proper effect on the potions made from them.

The planets themselves were associated with specific illnesses, and more recently with the glandular system – particularly the endocrine glands that release hormones into the blood. The Sun, for instance, which traditionally rules the heart, back and spinal column, is now associated with the thymus, connected with the immunisation of the body against bacteria. The Moon is associated with the breasts and the whole alimentary system has to do with the food system. Venus, always known to affect the throat and kidneys, is now also connected with the parathyroids, which control the calcium level in the blood. And Mars, associated throughout the ages with the sexual impulse, acts also on the urogenital system and gonads, or sex glands.

There is plenty of evidence that doctors still find astrology extremely useful. This book is not technical enough to show clearly how astrology is being used in medicine throughout the world. But it is.

There are many medieval drawings and paintings which associate various parts of the human body with the various planets and Signs. (The one on the right is an entertaining example, with the Arian ram sitting like a puppy-dog on the head and the Capricornian goat across the knees.) These associations, among the oldest in the history of astrology, were used in medicine and can of course be used in making love. The susceptibility to touch of body areas differs from person to person, and season to season, and can clearly be associated with the position of the planets within the Signs in a person's Birth Chart and the movement of the planets in the sky at the present time.

Very little real study has been given to this area of astrology: it is fun, and contributes to a happy love-relationship, to note for oneself how a loved one reacts to the sense of touch in connection with the Birth Chart. Here is a rough check-list of Signs and their associated parts of the body. The polarities – opposite Signs – often react the same, which is why planets are linked in pairs.

Gemini/Sagittarius: arms, shoulders
Leo/Aquarius: spine and back

Just as the traditional connections between the Zodiac Signs and various parts of the body can be used in medicine, so too can they be used in love-making to ensure a happier and more fulfilled partnership.

Libra/Aries: kidneys
Scorpio/Taurus: sexual organs
Capricorn/Cancer: knees and teeth
Pisces/Virgo: feet
Aries/Libra: head
Taurus/Scorpio: throat and neck
Cancer/Capricorn: stomach, breasts
Virgo/Pisces: nervous system
Sagittarius/Gemini: hips and thighs
Aquarius/Leo: shins, ankles, veins

Additionally, the Sun rules the heart, back and spinal column; the Moon rules the breasts; Mars, the genital area; Venus, the throat; and Saturn, the skin's surface.

The gods in love

'The Gods are humans under the microscope' —MOLIERE

The spry gods of Greece and Rome had many adventures, celebrated by various writers – some of them concerned with war, revenge, murder, but a great many too about love, including some of the most famous love-stories ever: of Cupid and Psyche, for instance.

The Greek god most familiar to us still figures on most Valentine cards in the 1970s, but in fact is the oldest god of all – Cupid, whose name is the Latin version of the Greek god of love, Eros. Eros was hatched from the 'world-egg', and was the first of the gods for the very simple reason that without him none of the others could have been born! A wild and beautiful boy, he showed no respect for age, sex or appearance, and flew about shooting the darts of love into unsuspecting mortals and gods alike, infecting them with love as freely as we, today, catch influenza.

Aphrodite, later known as Venus, was goddess of desire, and rose naked from the foam of the sea to ride on a scallop shell to Cyprus, where she lived ever after. She wore a magic girdle which made everyone fall in love with its owner; she had many affairs with gods and humans, and was the cause of much jealousy and squabbling in heaven.

Zeus, father of heaven, set no particularly good example where morals were concerned; with a vast appetite for love affairs, he had no hesitation in using his magic powers to seduce any woman who appealed to him, by turning himself into animal or bird or insect in order to gain access to her – for instance, he turned himself into a perfect replica of the hero Amphitryon in order to make love to the beautiful Alcmene, Amphitryon's wife; their son, Hercules, was one of the most famous of all mythical heroes.

Both the delights and horrors of love are celebrated in the myths: some of the women in these stories are vicious (like Lamia, who made love to young men only to suck their blood as they lay asleep), some beautiful and patient (like Phyllis, changed into an almond-tree as she

Aphrodite, goddess of physical love, worshipped as mistress of all things, was mother of Eros, god of romance, later known as Cupid.

waited for her lover Acamas, which blossomed as he embraced her), and some spirited as Leda, who led the pursuing Zeus a pretty dance – becoming first a fish (he chased her as a beaver), then various other swift-running beasts, and finally a wild goose. But he became a swan, and finally caught her; their child, born out of the hyacinth-coloured egg, was Helen of Troy, whose beauty caused the Trojan wars.

Every country in the world has its stories of fairy-tale and legend, many of them dealing with that most fascinating of all subjects, love. The most numerous are the Greek myths, which contain the plot of every love story ever told, later, by modern

Apollo, god of light, lord of music and son, has a special relationship with astrology, for he was also the Homeric god of prophesy.

writers. They grew out of the Greek idea that love-making was a major form of amusement, and that the organisation of a love affair could provide hours of innocent fun. What the gods forgot, of course, was that one trifles with love at one's peril. Their punishment was not prosecution for rape or obscenity, but the pain and suffering they inflicted on themselves by their lack of consideration for each other and the unfortunate mortals who were their victims. Many of their victims did achieve immortality, in the constellations of the night sky, where today shine the Pleiades, for for instance, turned into doves, then stars, to protect them from Orion, the handsomest man on earth!

Love in fact and fiction

The reality and the ideal

Real people have all the signs and all the planets in their Birth Charts; fictional characters sometimes seem to have the attributes of one particular sign only. In the following pages, we look at both living and fictional characters, and at how their astrological personality is revealed in their love-life.

Madame Bovary

Gustave Flaubert published his novel *Madame Bovary* in 1857. It shocked the men of France . . . and made their wives feel that no other author had so understood a woman's secret longings.

Emma Bovary, the daughter of a farmer, educated in a convent, was dissatisfied with her life as the wife of the worthy but boring Dr Charles Bovary in the dull, provincial town of Yonvonne-l'Abbaye. Bored to distraction, she fell in love with the young and handsome Leon Dupuis, a poetic but poor lawyer's clerk. Neither of them declared their love and, believing that she would never care for him, Leon left Yonvonne for Rouen to finish his studies.

When the equally handsome, coarse but shrewd landowner Rodolphe Boulanger came to consult Dr Bovary, Emma turned to him, and he was quick to take advantage of her typical Libran discontent and gullibility and seduce her. Hopelessly in love, she beseeched Rodolphe to elope with her; but, shunning the complications, he left town.

Emma, ill, was devotedly nursed by her husband. But when he took her to Rouen and to the opera, and they re-met Leon, she renewed her affair, this time with the utmost passion. Her extravagance and carelessness over money (another negative Libran trait) led her husband into debt. When the bailiffs moved in and prepared to sell the furniture, Leon declined to steal money to help her, and Rodolphe swore that he did not have any to lend. All chance of agreeable Libran comfort gone, she persuaded her husband's assistant to give her the key to his laboratory and took arsenic. Charles Bovary, seeing her die, soon perished of grief.

Reading the story, every Frenchwoman thought of herself as Emma Bovary, and most astrologers saw in her a warning of the negative effects of Libran influence – if also of the romantic and idealistic attitude to life which is so charming.

Don Juan

The character of Don Juan – surely the typical Geminian lover – was invented in the 16th century by Gabriel Tellez, and his amorous adventures have been written about by many people – including Mozart, Byron, Shaw and Browning.

Mozart used the best-known adventure of Don Juan for his opera *Don Giovanni*, in which Juan, the most famous lover in Spain, seduces the beautiful Donna Anna and kills her father, the noble Commandant of the Knights of Malta, in a duel. Juan goes on to other conquests, accompanied by his comic servant Leporello, who keeps a tally of his master's affairs. He makes love to most of the beautiful women of Spain and eventually returns to Seville, where, noticing a statue to the memory of the dead Commandant in the main square, he recklessly

Emma Bovary, Don Juan and Henry Higgins (top to bottom) illustrate the negative characters of the idealized Sign portraits beside them: the frivolous, discontented Libran, the reckless, fickle Geminian and the tactless, unconventional Sagittarian.

invites it to dine with him. To his surprise – and Leporello's terror – the statue accepts. At the appointed hour, the great stone figure pounds at the door of Juan's house. Fearfully Leporello lets it in, and, when Juan advances to meet it, the statue grasps his hand in an ice-cold grip and drags the reckless and amoral lover down to the flames of hell.

Byron's Don Juan is a more sympathetic figure, and perhaps even more Geminian in his rapid progress from lady to lady. After an affair with Donna Julia in Seville when he is only fifteen, Juan is sent abroad by his mother. After an adventurous shipwreck (his spaniel and his tutor eaten by hungry sailors!), he is cast away on a Greek island and rescued by Haidée, the lovely daughter of a Greek pirate. Their passionate affair is ended by her father and she dies of grief. Juan, exiled, becomes a slave in Constantinople, bought by a sultana who has fallen in love with him. Escaping to Russia, he becomes the favourite of the Empress; then, in England, has many more affairs. Juan – and maybe Gemini – may well be fickle in love, but never bored.

Henry Higgins
Henry Higgins, created by George Bernard Shaw in his play *Pygmalion*, became world-famous when the play became the musical *My Fair Lady* and was later filmed. Rex Harrison, the most famous actor to play Higgins, certainly gave the role the correct Sagittarian flavour, presenting Higgins as an optimistic, idealistic, somewhat short-tempered professor who gambles on turning the little Cockney flower-girl Eliza into 'a lady'. Shaw did not write a happy ending for his play: Higgins and Eliza did not fall in love. But generations of play- and film-goers have suspected that, after the curtain fell, neither he nor she found it possible to resist the power that seems to be drawing them together. Would she be able to cure his temper, tactlessness, exaggeration? If so, it would be worth it!

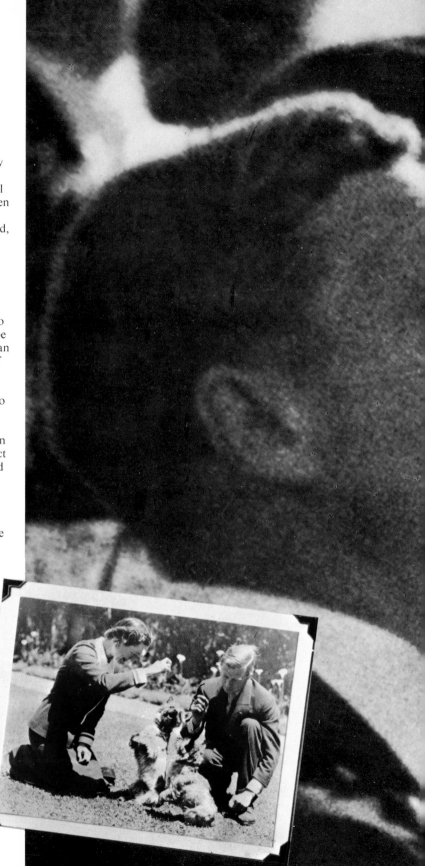

Love in fact and fiction

The Windsors

Edward, eldest son of King George V, was brought up to be fully conscious of the duties of kingship. It was taken for granted that sooner or later he would marry a 'suitable' bride – a member, perhaps, of another European royal house, fit to be Queen. In 1936, when he succeeded to the throne as Edward VIII, he was still unmarried, and there was naturally much speculation about the possible future Queen.

In England, Edward was a popular young man who seemed to lead an enjoyable and relaxed social life; no particular woman was thought to be a special favourite. But the American Press was beginning to take note of his friendship with Mrs Simpson, the wife of an American business-man, and it soon became obvious to everyone but the British that Edward and Wallis Simpson were very much in love. Eventually, when it became impossible to hide the fact any longer, the British Press printed the story, and there began an agonising time for the lovers. In a truly Cancerian fashion, Edward loved his family and was conscious of his duty to them; but, equally, he was faithful to his love for Mrs Simpson, and announced that he would marry her as soon as her divorce was through.

The King's forward-looking and radical opinions (he had an Aquarian Ascendant) had already made him unpopular with many politicians, and, after much heart-searching, he decided that since they would obviously never permit him to marry Mrs Simpson and remain King, he would abdicate. So he left England forever – married his love and lived happily with her until his death in 1972.

The King who gave up a throne for the sake of love : Edward the VIII's sign was Cancer His sense of duty was overwhelmed by his feelings for Mrs. Wallis Simpson. She is a Gemini with Venus in Cancer.

Elizabeth Barrett, a sensitive and beautiful Piscean, lacked the spirit to rebel against the harshness of her father, who, because he thought her seriously ill, forbade her to have any male friends and kept her shut up in a bedroom of his house in Wimpole Street, London. But Mr Barrett reckoned without the handsome,

sturdy Taurean Robert Browning, a popular and well-known poet. Browning had read a book of poems that Elizabeth had published and wrote to her. Then, greatly daring, she invited him to call.

It soon became clear that he wanted to marry her. But her father had forbidden her to marry and she thought that she was genuinely ill. When doctors declared that Italy would be best for her health, her father refused to consider the idea. But Robert immediately proposed to marry her and take her to Florence. So one morning in September 1846, Elizabeth Barrett walked out of her father's house,

became Mrs Robert Browning in a nearby church and returned home as though nothing had happened. A week later with Robert she crossed to France, then travelled south.

Pisceans can tend to be weak-willed and indecisive – but Robert's Taurean assurance and affection made Elizabeth strong. She wrote for him some of the best love poems in the English language (see page 40).

After they were both dead, their love letters were published – the story of two people who rescued each other from loneliness and who (not least because of their astrological compatibility) found lasting love.

Beauty and the Beast

'Once upon a time. . .' Thus begin so many of the world's most beautiful stories, and *Beauty and the Beast*, retold by Mme de Villeneuve 200 years ago (though the story itself is much older), is one of the loveliest.

Once upon a time, then, there lived in France a rich merchant whose fleets sailed the seven seas, bringing home great treasures. He had three handsome sons and three beautiful daughters, the most beautiful of whom was so lovely that no one called her anything but 'Beauty'. When disaster came, and her father lost all his money, she looked upon it as a great adventure, and, while her sisters grumbled, she looked after the family like a mother.

One day her father, on his travels, took refuge from a storm in an apparently empty castle, where he was fed and given rich new clothes by an invisible host. As he left, he plucked a rose to take home for Beauty – and immediately a hideous Beast appeared and threatened to kill him unless within three months he brought him his youngest daughter. Though her father protested, Beauty insisted that the bargain should be kept, and in three months' time she was taken to the Beast's castle, where she was given a fine suite of rooms, handsome clothes and good food.

At first Beauty was frightened by the Beast, but gradually found him to be kind and gentle. Each day, he asked her to marry him; each day, though her compassionate Piscean heart sympathised with him, she refused.

When she begged permission to visit her family, the Beast reluctantly consented. She took them many presents, and her sisters were intensely jealous when they saw her fine clothes and heard stories of the luxurious castle where she lived. Hoping to make the Beast angry with her, they persuaded her to stay longer than the week he had allowed her. But Beauty had a dream: she saw the garden of the Beast's castle, and in it, beneath a rose tree, he lay dying.

She rushed back to the castle and there, as in her dream, he lay – he had starved himself for love of her, believing that she had deserted him. 'O Beauty!' he said, 'it is better so; when I am dead, you shall live here, untroubled by my ugliness!'

At this, Beauty's heart was touched. 'Dear Beast,' she said, 'do not die! I know that your soul is pure and good, and I want nothing better than that you shall be my husband.'

And at once before her lay not the Beast but a handsome and noble Prince. He had been changed into a beast by a witch, to remain so until he could find a beautiful young girl who would marry him.

And so, of course, they were married: the Prince and his Beauty lived happily ever after. Her father became the Prince's Chamberlain, in charge of all his rich domains, and her brothers became his companions and friends. As for the jealous sisters, they were changed to stone and stood at the entrance to his palace to wait until their souls became as pure and loving as that of their sister, Beauty. For all we know, they are standing there still.

Madame Butterfly

Madame Butterfly is perhaps the favourite love story in opera. Puccini took it from a play by the American author David Belasco.

Lieutenant Pinkerton, of the US Navy, has fallen in love with the beautiful Japanese girl Cho-Cho-San whom he calls 'Butterfly', and their marriage has been arranged by a marriage broker named Goro. The American consul in Nagasaki does his best to persuade Pinkerton that he is making a mistake, but despite his warnings – and the fury of Butterfly's uncle, a priest, and her other relations when they learn that she has become a Christian for Pinkerton's sake – the marriage ceremony is performed, and after one of the most beautiful love duets in opera they go together to their new home on the hill above the harbour.

Soon after the wedding Pinkerton is recalled to America, and for three years Butterfly lives alone on the hill – alone, that is, except for her faithful maid Suzuki and the young son she has borne Pinkerton. Goro tries to persuade her to marry the rich Prince Yamadori (under Japanese law she could divorce Pinkerton for desertion), but she refuses: she is an American citizen.

The idealized Cancerian – and Madame Butterfly.

Then a gun-shot from the harbour announces the arrival of a ship. It is the *Abraham Lincoln* – Pinkerton's ship. Butterfly makes the house ready, and waits until morning looking over the hill for her husband's approach. When he comes, Butterfly is asleep, but Zuzuki greets him – and sees a woman in the garden outside. Sheepishly, Pinkerton admits that it is his American wife, Kate, and asks Suzuki to tell Butterfly that she is willing to adopt the child. Butterfly appears and guesses the truth. She will hand over her son in half a hour, she tells Kate. Then, sending Suzuki away, she takes down her father's sword, with its motto 'Death with honour is better than life with dishonour'. And with it, the faithful Cancerian kills herself. . . .

Falstaff

Falstaff in love is almost a contradiction in terms, for all this typical Taurean's affection was directed inwards – to himself. He lived a life of lazy pleasure, well-known in the taverns of London, and well-known to the innkeeper's wives, daughters and serving-girls. But it was difficult to dislike him, for he had all the Taurean's affectionate good-humour, as well as his addiction to good food and drink.

But in *The Merry Wives of Windsor*, Shakespeare gives him his come-uppance. Falstaff sends two identical love letters to Mrs Ford and Mrs Page. Discovering this, they have their own back – first by Mrs Ford, pretending to hear her husband, hiding Falstaff in a linen-basket, and then tipping him into the Thames; then by Mrs Page, disguising him as a woman whom her husband soundly beats.

James Bond

Reading the adventures of James Bond, it is difficult not to reach the conclusion that his creator, Ian Fleming, conceived him as the absolute Scorpio – especially where his attitude to women is concerned. By the end of each novel, Bond has had yet another affair with yet another beautiful girl, even more memorable than the last, extremely passionate, yet in the end ephemeral.

Bond has all Scorpio's usual magnetic charm. Immensely good-looking, and with true Scorpionic power over the opposite sex, he brings his high energy level to bear not only on the adventure in which he's concerned but on the love-making that always accompanies it. This is not entirely free of the violence and cruelty, which is also a part of his life – and which, to be fair, is often used against him.

All the Bond books (like less popular spy thrillers) present their hero with a problem, and Scorpios are at their most intense and unshakeable when working on the small details of a large problem. Long before Ian Fleming thought of Bond, Scorpios were nicknamed 'the investigators' by astrologers. They love a 'cause' – in Bond's case, his country.

Bond (above) evinces the Scorpio's magnetic charm.

Falstaff (below) – example of the Taurean's good humour.

glamorous, remote Aquarius has a say as well, for it was rising when she was born. Aquarius is often prominent in the Charts of theatre people, and while Taurus is one of the cosier, more contented Signs, loving creature comforts, lovely possessions, it also needs security. So many Taureans tend to become complacent, and once settled will take life easily, not wanting to be disturbed. This couldn't be less so in Dame Margot's case: she works every day of her life in the most physically demanding of all careers. She has had to make many sacrifices for it, and may well have suffered some conflict, especially when deciding what relative places in her life her career and her husband should take. This will have come to a crisis when Roberto de Arias was permanently disabled in an assassination attempt. Dame Margot's Taurean instinct would have been to drop everything, to be

A full analysis of a complete Birth Chart will often run for several thousand words; but on these pages in a few words we indicate some of the astrological reasons for some traits in the characters of five well-known people.

Gloria Swanson, screen vamp of the 1930s, has Venus – the love planet – in cool, distant Aquarius. Sexy Mars in sensuous Cancer also contributes a great deal to her personality in private life; and as for her 'glamour' – well, Venus and Mars are 'in aspect' (in astrology, planets are 'in aspect' when there are certain specific angular distances between them, as they are seen from Earth). Though in this case the aspect is only a *quincunx* (150°, and a fairly weak aspect), because Mars is Miss Swanson's Sun ruler, any influences it receives from other planets will be most pronounced.

Aries is Miss Swanson's Sun Sign, and Sagittarius was the Sign on the eastern horizon at the moment of her birth. Both are powerful, lively 'fire' Signs, and have made her passionate,

enthusiastic and emotional. However, Saturn was rising in Sagittarius when she was born, and the powerful influence of that planet will always have held down a great deal of her natural fire, making it smoulder rather than crackle.

Fame, fortune and rapport with the general public is shown by the position of the Moon in Libra and in conjunction with the Midheaven, the area of the Chart influencing the career. It's very common for famous people to have the Moon on or near this particular angle of their Birth Charts. It also shows that they can in their turn exert some kind of influence over the masses, just as Miss Swanson did through her whole image and seductive quality.

The Moon was in a similar position in the sky at the time when **Dame Margot Fonteyn** was born – high in the Tenth House; and here again we have fame, with the love and admiration of a great public. Dame Margot's Sun Sign is Taurus – ruled by Venus, and a very romantic and loving Sign. But in contrast,

34

constantly with him, giving him all her time and affection. But Taurus is, too, essentially an extremely practical Sign, and she decided to work on for his benefit and our delight if sometimes to her own distress.

There is some doubt about the exact time of Dame Margot's birth: if she had been born slightly later than 2.15 a.m., G.M.T., her Rising Sign would have been Pisces rather than Aquarius. The Piscean attributes of impracticality and capacity for sacrifice could have overwhelmed her in that case, and she might well have retired, uncaring for the need for security.

Taurus has the reputation of being the best-looking of all the Signs, and Aquarius is impregnated with glamour. Both these qualities are lavishly bestowed on Dame Margot, and in a personal encounter are even more shattering than when she is seen across the footlights: her huge, expressive eyes, quick changes of expression, distant, cool but dynamic glamour are quintessentially Aquarian – and all are softened by the Taurean Sun, and by Venus (in Cancer when she was born). And the Sun and Mars, in conjunction – a powerful aspect – give her energy and enormous will to work.

The Moon was again high in the sky and in the Tenth House of the Birth Chart when **John Lennon** was born; and again, fame, fortune and an enormous influence over masses of people resulted. John's Sun Sign is Libra and he has Aries rising, which make him passionate, and probably more romantic than he may care to admit. But because Venus is in Virgo, he is also extremely critical of the women in his life. The two 'gas giants' of the Zodiac, Jupiter and Saturn, were in conjunction when he was born, which will help him to plod on and work hard – though they may also mean that he can never rest content, something he perhaps needs to watch in his personal as well as public life.

Queen Elizabeth II is a Taurean,

with Capricorn rising, and her Sun-ruler, Venus, in Pisces – making her a very affectionate and warm wife and mother. The Capricornian sense of duty is manifest in her whole life, and there is no need to ask (as one would with a private person) how it influences her attitude to her career! The sensible qualities of Taurus and Capricorn combine to make her conscientious, practical and constructive. Her ruling planet is Saturn (for it rules Capricorn), and it was high in the sky when she was born – in conjunction with her Midheaven, which has an enormously powerful bearing on incidents over which we have no control – such as the very incident which, though it happened when she was a child, resulted in her becoming Queen. Any astrologer looking at her Birth Chart, even if he did not know who the subject was, would say that here was someone who had had to make considerable sacrifices, and carry a heavy burden of responsibility. The time the Queen can spend with her Geminian husband and four delightful children must be of enormous value in helping her carry her great responsibilities with reassuring calmness and charm.

The Sun, Mercury and Mars were all in Pisces when **Elizabeth Taylor** was born. Venus and Uranus were exactly together in Aries, and Libra was rising over the eastern horizon. When Libra is the Rising Sign, perhaps the Libran need for a permanent relationship is even

greater than when it is the Sun Sign, and very often it is true that the person concerned needs vitally to be able to relate to a partner. Miss Taylor's (perhaps unconscious) need for a partnership may have been the motive for her early marriage: the romantic notion of being 'in love with love' could be familiar to her. Pluto, planet of disruptive change, was high in the sky when she was born, and its effect on her life has been fairly obvious. Success has often been accompanied by tragedy and unhappiness. But eventually came her marriage to Richard Burton. Throughout this book you will find references to the 'polarity' of certain Signs, and there is often a specially good relationship between people whose Signs are opposite across the Zodiac. This is true with the Burtons, for his Sun Sign is Virgo. This need not mean that life is easy or simple for them as a couple; but at its best it will be very, very good.

Miss Taylor's passion, glamour and intensity, her sensuously emotional appeal, show abundantly in her Chart, with Moon in Scorpio, Venus in conjunction with Uranus in Aries, and Mars with the Sun in Pisces. All this may sound technical, but will make any astrologer mop his brow at the thought of that planetary dynamism!

Astrological miscellany of love

Putting emotions into words

One of the pleasures, you might even say one of the duties, of being in love is to *celebrate* the fact. And it's not difficult. When you're in love, bells are ringing, the skies seem always blue, the stars are always shining, moon rhymes with June, and just to be alive is celebration enough. . . .

On the other hand, not many lovers are particularly good at expressing their feelings, and shared experience often has to be a substitute for the joy a painter might put into a picture,

a composer into a serenade, a poet into a poem. We see a film together, and the love story on the screen becomes part of our love story; we hear a tune, and ever after it is 'our tune'; we read a poem, and its lines say exactly what we would say, if we could find the words.

Poets strive to describe what, for the rest of us, is indescribable. The emotion of love is one of the most difficult things in the world to express in anything other than a look

or a gesture, so it is not surprising that most poets have, at some time, written love poetry. Here are a few lines from some of the world's greatest love poetry. Read them – alone or together. They will not only enrich your own experience, they will perhaps open the door a little on the whole idea of love – what it means to love tenderly, passionately, hopelessly. Through them, you can share the joy of other men and women, making your own experience part of a *world* of lovers.

We love being in love, that's the truth on't.
                    – W. M. THACKERAY

Love goes toward love, as schoolboys from their books;
But love from love, toward school with heavy looks.
                    – WILLIAM SHAKESPEARE

Love is the wisdom of the fool and the folly of the wise.
                    – SAMUEL JOHNSON

Youth's the season made for joys,
Love is then our duty.
                    – JOHN GAY

Quoth John to Joan

Quoth John to Joan, will thou have me?
  I prithee now, wilt? and I'll marry thee
My cow, my calf, my house, my rents,
And all my lands and tenements:
  Oh, say, my Joan, will not that do?
  I cannot come every day to woo.

To marry I would have thy consent,
  But faith I never could compliment;
I can say nought but 'Hoy, gee ho!'
Words that belong to cart and plough.
  Oh, say, my Joan, will not that do?
  I cannot come every day to woo.

                    ANON

Rosaline

Like to the clear in highest sphere
  Where all imperial glory shines,
Of self-same colour is her hair
  Whether unfolded or in twines
    Heigh ho, fair Rosaline!
Her eyes are sapphires set in snow,
  Resembling heaven by every wink;
The gods do fear when as they glow.
  And I do tremble when I think
    Heigh ho, would she were mine!

Her cheeks are like the blushing cloud
  That beautifies Aurora's face,
Or like the silver crimson shroud
  That Phoebus' smiling looks doth grace:
    Heigh ho, fair Rosaline!
Her lips are like two budded roses
  Whom ranks of lilies neighbour night,
Within whose bounds she balm encloses
  Apt to entice a deity:
    Heigh ho, would she were mine!

THOMAS LODGE, 1558–1625

No Limits

I cannot exist without you. I am forgetful
of everything but seeing you again – my
life seems to stop there – I see no further.
You have absorbed me. I have a sensation
at the present moment as though I was
dissolving – I should be exquisitely
miserable without the hope of soon
seeing you. I should be afraid to separate
myself far from you. . . . I have no limit
not to my love. Love is my religion.
I could die for that. I could die for you.

– JOHN KEATS, 1795–1821

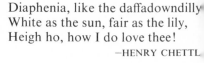

Diaphenia, like the daffadowndilly
White as the sun, fair as the lily,
Heigh ho, how I do love thee!
— HENRY CHETTL

But to see her was to love her,
Love but her, and love for ever.
— ROBERT BURNS

O Mistress Mine

O mistress mine, where are you roaming?
O stay and hear, your true love's coming
   That can sing both high and low.
Trip no further, pretty sweeting;
Journeys end in lovers meeting,
   Every wise man's son doth know.

What is love? 'Tis not hereafter:
Present mirth hath present laughter,
   What's to come is still unsure.
In delay there lies no plenty –
Then come kiss me, sweet-and-twenty:
   Youth's a stuff will not endure.

— WILLIAM SHAKESPEARE

Next to being married, a girl likes to
be crossed in love a little now and then.
— JANE AUSTEN

Love in Thy Youth

Love in thy youth, fair maid; be wise,
  Old time will make thee colder,
And though each morning new arise
  Yet we each day grow older.

Thou as heaven art fair and young,
  Thine eyes like twin stars shining:
But ere another day be sprung
  All these will be declining.

Then winter comes with all his fears
  And all thy sweets shall borrow;
Too late then wilt thou shower thy tears,
  And I too late shall sorrow.

— ANON

Sweet, Let Me Go

Sweet, let me go! sweet, let me go!
What do you mean to vex me so?
Cease your pleading force!
Do you think thus to extort
    remorse?
Now, now, no more! alas; you
    overbear me,
And I would cry,
- but some would hear, I fear me.

— ANON

The Kiss

O that joy so soon should waste!
  Or so sweet a bliss
  As a kiss
Might not for ever last!
So sugared, so melting, so soft,
  so delicious,
  The dew that lies on roses,
  When the moon herself discloses,
Is not so precious.
O, rather than it would I smother,
Were I to taste such another;
  It should be my wishing
  That I might die kissing.

– BEN JONSON, 1572–1637

How Do I Love Thee?

How do I love thee? Let me count the ways.
I love thee to the depth and breadth and height
My soul can reach, when feeling out of sight
For the ends of Being and ideal Grace.
I love thee to the level of every day's
Most quiet need, by sun and candle-light.
I love thee freely, as men strive for right;
I love thee purely, as they turn from praise.
I love thee with the passion put to use
In my old griefs, and with my childhood's faith.
I love thee with a love I seemed to lose
With my lost saints – I love thee with the breath,
Smiles, tears, of all my life! – and, if God choose,
I shall but love thee better after death.

– ELIZABETH BARRETT BROWNING

Remember

Remember me when I am gone away,
Gone far away into the silent land;
When you can no more hold me by the hand,
Nor I half turn to go yet turning stay.
Remember me when no more day by day
You tell me of our future that you planned;
Only remember me; you understand
It will be late to counsel then or pray.
Yet if you should forget me for a while
And afterwards remember, do not grieve:
For if the darkness and corruption leave
A vestige of the thoughts that once I had,
Better by far you should forget and smile
Than that you should remember and be sad.

– CHRISTINA ROSSETTI, 1830–1894

Let's Now Take Our Time

Let's now take our time
While we're in our prime,
And old, old age is afar off:
For the evil, evil days
Will come on apace
Before we can be aware of.

– ROBERT HERRICK, 1591–1674

Sleep is still most perfect, in spite of hygienists,
when it is shared with a beloved. The warmth, the
security and peace of soul, the utter comfort from
the touch of the other, knits the sleep, so that it
takes the body and soul completely in its healing.

– D. H. LAWRENCE, 1885–1930

ove rules the court, the camp, the grove,
nd men below, and saints above;
or love is heaven, and heaven is love.
          – SIR WALTER SCOTT

ove sought is good, but given unsought is
etter.

          – WILLIAM SHAKESPEARE

No, there's nothing half so sweet in life
As love's young dream.
          – THOMAS MOORE

The herbs of love
Seasoning the food of love

From time immemorial, man has used herbs as medicines. As Shakespeare made the Friar in *Romeo and Juliet* say:

Naught so vile that on the earth doth live
But to the earth some special good
doth give.

The men and women of Shakespeare's age would have recognised that as a fact. And men and women used herbs, too, in love – as aphrodisiacs, to beautify the body and to encourage sexual health. The most thorough study of herbs and their uses was made by the 17th century astrologer-physician Nicholas Culpeper, whose *Herbal*, published in the 1640s, is still in print.

Culpeper was an astrologer as well as a herbalist; in his office in Red Lion Street, London, he treated patients and between-times worked on his book about herbs and their uses.

The knowledge he collected together in the *Herbal* was not all his own: he used material first set down by Arabian astrologers hundreds of years before his own time.
He associated all herbs with their ruling planets and suggested that 'such as are astrologers (and indeed none else are fit to make physicians)' should gather the herbs when the planet governing them was rising, setting, or immediately overhead, and with the Moon 'in good aspect'. He also gives careful instructions for their use; and today anyone experimenting in the use of herbs as medicine should take the precaution of consulting an acknowledged herbalist before preparing and taking potions, some of which may be poisonous.

Culpeper, though he pointed out some herbs which 'stir up venery or bodily lust', kept carefully away from

the whole question of aphrodisiacs – which indeed remain controversial and dangerous. Powders prepared from the insect cantharides (the notorious 'Spanish Fly') can cause serious damage to the gastro-intestinal system, which it inflames; yohimbine, from the bark of the African yohimbé tree, can cripple.

There are more innocent aphrodisiacs, though whether they work or not is questionable. The sweet potato, chestnuts, onions, eringo and asparagus are all pleasant to eat, whether or not they have any effect in the courts of love Carrots, now served at almost every dinner, were in Elizabethan days said to be 'great furtherers of Venus her pleasure and of love's delights'! But here are a few of Culpeper's original recommendations – none of them, we suppose, very likely to harm and perhaps equally unlikely to help.

Asparagus (Jupiter) 'Being taken fasting several mornings together, stirreth up bodily lust in man or woman.'

Garden Mint (Venus) 'The juice taken in vinegar stirs up venery or bodily lust.'

Mustard (Mars) 'Whenever a strong, stimulating medicine is wanted to act upon the nerves and recall the natural heat, there is none preferable to mustard-seed.'

Lettuce (Moon) 'It abates bodily lust, represses venerous dreams, being outwardly applied to the testicles with a little camphire.'

Onion (Mars) 'Increases sperm, especially the seed.'
Arrach (Venus in Scorpio) 'It makes barren women fruitful.'

Cat-Mint (Venus) 'By frequent use it takes away barrenness. . .'

Ladies' Mantle (Venus) 'Helps women who have over-flagging breasts, causing them to grow less hard, both when drunk and outwardly applied.'

Cowslips (Venus in Aries) 'Our city dames know well enough the ointment or distilled water of it adds to beauty, or restores it when it is lost.'

As long as man has recognized the fact that at some time or another he will fall in love, he has attempted to look into the future for the face of the girl he will one day meet. The same is of course true of the woman, who never tires of seeking for the 'tall, dark stranger' that fortune-tellers traditionally see around every corner. Besides astrology, many other forms of 'divination' have been used – from palmistry and the tarot to reading tea-leaves, looking at reflections in oil or water and the Chinese *I Ching*.

In palmistry, the lines on the hand are interpreted to show the way life has been shaped in the past and may be shaped in the future. The 'love-line' can be strong or weak, intact or broken, showing the course of true (or false) love as it may unfold. Palmistry has a literature and a tradition equalled only by astrology, and has sometimes been used with great accuracy by qualified practitioners (who, in Great Britain, may have passed an examination).

In the Tarot, a pack of cards showing various symbols (some devised in ancient Egypt) is dealt and interpreted. Cards include The Lover (representing physical love, marriage) The Queen of Swords (a dark wicked woman) and The Cavalier (a young dark man). Much depends on the interpreter. . . .

The *I Ching* or *Book of Changes*, compiled centuries before Christ, is a book of 'mottos', the 'motto' revealing the course of love or life being chosen by the casting of arrow stalks or coins. The *I Ching* will never give a definite answer, but will indicate a course of action.

There are many lesser-known methods of looking in the future, including *capnomancy* (divination by the smoke from burning poppy seeds), *onychomancy* (by reflections from the oiled fingernails of a virgin), *lithomancy* (by the sound made when two stones are struck together), *hippomancy* (by the neighing of sacred horses) and *ichthyomancy* (by examining the

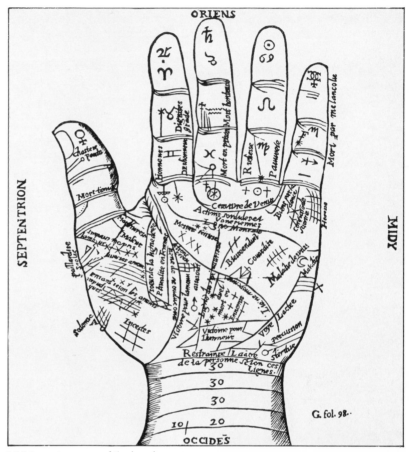

A 17th century map of the hand (above). Important lines include the life-line, head-line, heart-line, line-of-fortune, line-of-the-liver; the 'bumps' are named after the planets.
Pietro Longhi shows in his painting (right) an 18th century girl offering her palm to a street-palmist.

entrails of a fish). Means like the flight of birds, sacred smoke and the entrails of sacred beasts have been used for many centuries.

In Elizabethan England, and earlier, many witches invented spells which allegedly could show the face and body of an unknown lover: they depended, it seems, almost entirely on the faith of the person asking the question, and sometimes on wishful thinking. It is true that in all forms of divination the person seeking to know something about himself and his future must believe in the means he has chosen and in the person of whom he is asking the questions.

Where's your Venus?

The emotional side of love

Venus influences the capacity for love and affection, Mars a man's or a woman's sexual response. The effects of Venus are strongest when it is in Taurus or Libra. If your Venus is in the same sign as your Sun, what you read about your love-life under your Zodiac sign ought to be accurate; if Venus falls in a different sign, this gives another dimension to the expression of your love.

In order to find out where your own or your partner's Venus is, turn to the astrological table on page 46. First find your year of birth on the top line of the table and then your month of birth at the lefthand side of the chart (1 = January, 2 = February, etc.). The table shows in which sign of the Zodiac Venus was on the first of each month and also any date during that month on which it moved to another sign. For instance, if you look at the table, you will see that in January 1947 Venus was in Scorpio on the first of the month, and moved into Sagittarius on 6th January.

VENUS THROUGH THE SIGNS

Venus in Aires ♈

A warm and affectionate man or woman; probably very emotional, but with fiery, positive emotion. Best summed up as ardent and true – but watch out for selfishness, especially if the Sun sign is Aries when, although there will be kindness, there may also be self-seeking tendencies.

Venus in Taurus ♉

Here is someone who will lavish affection on a partner, and contribute much to the development of a relationship. Possessiveness is bound to be present, and the loved one will almost inevitably be thought of as 'mine', in much the same way as any other treasured possession.

Venus in Gemini ♊

Those who have Venus in this sign will enjoy their relationships, and perhaps take them rather lightly. There is a strong possibility that they will have 'more than one string to their bow', and they can find themselves in love with two people at the same time.

Venus in Cancer ♋

This placing contributes much tenderness and a strong tendency to look after the loved one. A certain claustrophobic feeling may be in evidence, because the person is so cherishing or sentimental. They may also dwell in the past too much. A high emotional level is very likely.

Venus in Leo ♌

Love, affection and loyalty will be expressed in a grand and probably expensive way, especially if the Sun sign is Leo or Libra. There may be a tendency to dominate or rule the partner, and dramatic scenes are possible!

Venus in Virgo ♍

This tends to contribute over-critical, clinical or chaste tendencies, inhibiting a full, satisfactory expression of love; so conflict can occur, especially if the Sun sign is loving, romantic Libra. The need for a 'perfect' partner may be a root cause of difficulty in relationships.

Venus in Libra ♎

This placing indicates a whole-hearted romantic who is not a fully integrated person until he or she is enjoying a permanent relationship. If the Sun sign is Virgo, this will warm the matter-of-fact, practical Virgoan heart. Powerfully romantic and affectionate feelings are inevitable.

Venus in Scorpio ♏

Considerable intensity, emotion and intuition will be very evident in the expression of affection and feelings. Jealousy and possessiveness may mar the relationship, and a very 'black-and-white' attitude to love is very likely. These tendencies are modified if the Sun sign is Libra or Sagittarius.

Venus in Sagittarius ♐

This is definitely a lively position for Venus, and the overall attitude to love and relationships may not be too serious. More than one relationship is likely, and there is also an idealistic facet, which is very positive. Great warmth, affection and enthusiasm

will be fully expressed, however.

Venus in Capricorn ♑

Venus's influence in this sign is chilly, but once the barriers are broken one finds an extremely loyal, faithful, and dependable person. There will be few words of affection, but what is said is meant – especially if the Sun sign is Capricorn, rather than Sagittarius.

Venus in Aquarius ♒

This placing nearly always contributes a sort of filmstar glamour; if the Sun sign is Capricorn it may be a little difficult to come really close to that person – physically or emotionally, but especially emotionally. There is often a marked tendency towards platonic friendships rather than romantic relationships.

Venus in Pisces ♓

A kind, loving, willing slave who cannot do enough for one! Life could become blissfully romantic in an unorganized way. There should be very little difficulty in getting on with a 'Venus in Pisces', though emotions could well run rather high at times.

Right Mars Although essentially a Roman god, Mars is associated with the Greek god of war.

Below A detail from Sandro Botticelli's *The Birth of Venus,* in which the Roman goddess of love and beauty is shown rising from the sea.

Where's your Mars?

The way love finds expression

Mars is at its strongest in Aries, and in Scorpio.

Now turn to the table on page 47 and find out where your Mars (and your partner's!) were on your birthdates. The procedure is exactly the same as it was for finding your Venus, and the table will show you in which sign Mars was on the first day of any month, and the day or days in that month when it moved to another sign.

MARS THROUGH THE SIGNS

Mars in Aries ♈

Mars in Aries will contribute highly-sexed and passionate tendencies. The person will be demanding, but straightforward and good company. There will be no lack of enthusiasm, warmth and energy, and a general feeling that life is to be enjoyed.

Mars in Taurus ♉

An extremely passionate and highly-sexed man or woman. Feelings are usually slow to be roused, but once aroused sexual desire is strong. Jealousy and possessiveness can often creep into relationships. People with Mars in Taurus are extremely sensual, sexually demanding, and have expensive tastes.

Mars in Gemini ♊

Someone who may not want to become too deeply or emotionally involved with any one partner. A strong sexual desire is unusual, but there is great liking for innovation, variety and change in the style of love-making; many lovers are likely, with relationships kept at a superficial level.

Mars in Cancer ♋

Highly-sexed, but nevertheless roughness and boisterousness will be intensely disliked, so a gentle and sensitive approach is most advisable. Very strong feelings, emotions and intuitions are always present, and there is a tendency to cling to a relationship. In Cancer, Mars often increases fertility.

Mars in Leo ♌

Mars in Leo appreciates comfort and luxurious, aesthetically pleasing surroundings for sexual activities, and the result could be a highly sophisticated romp. There should undoubtedly be plenty of lively response to advances, but a slight hint of condescension may make one feel like an ever-grateful subject!

Mars in Virgo ♍

Virgo is purity personified, but Mars is all energy and sex: a contradiction in terms. Desire is certainly present, but the expression of it in a straightforward way may not be at all easy. Psychological difficulties as a result of conflict can cause repression, and deviation is possible.

Mars in Libra ♎

A languid attitude towards sex is very likely, and excuses may be made to put off the over-ardent lover. Once aroused, sensuousness will be evident; but, even so, sex has to be idealistic, colourful and beautiful – 'out of this world' rather than earthy!

Mars in Scorpio ♏

Mars in Scorpio, more than in any other sign, will make the individual extremely highly sexed. Unfortunately, jealousy and resentfulness can frequently blight relationships. Possibly the best way to combat this is to cultivate demanding interests, so that the excess of energy and emotion is positively directed.

Mars in Sagittarius ♐

A lively, unserious attitude to sex is likely. The man or woman with Mars in Sagittarius will enjoy relationships, but will make and break them easily, for freedom is highly prized. Those with Mars in Sagittarius will be passionate, but the grass will always seem greener on the other side!

Mars in Capricorn ♑

If those with Mars in Capricorn, caught up in the essential business of getting on in the world, can find the time to indulge in sexual relationships, they will be seething with passion at one moment, and an iceberg the next; but they will admire and identify with faithfulness and constancy.

Mars in Aquarius ♒

Having an affair with someone with Mars in Aquarius will be an all interesting experience, but togetherness, in the physical sense, may seem almost a necessary evil to them! They accept the fact that desires must be satisfied, but are somehow 'above it all'; passion is not really their scene.

Mars in Pisces ♓

Passion must always be combined with a colourful romanticism for those with Mars in Pisces. The emotional level is extremely high, but plain and simple earthy pleasures may not be enough to satisfy some highly individual escapist tendencies. An uncomplicated 'strong' partner will have a beneficial steadying influence.

Venus chart

Mars chart

The astrological Mars ephemeris tables give the zodiac sign position of Mars with the date of ingress into each sign. Each year column contains paired rows: a date row and a sign-symbol row.

1913–1928

	1913	1914	1915	1916	1917	1918	1919	1920	1921	1922	1923	1924	1925	1926	1927	1928
date	1 8	1 26	1	1 21	1 16	1	1 10	1 5 30	1 7	1 25	1 3	1 20	1 16	1	1 10	1 3 30
sign	≈ ♓	♐ ♑	♑ ≈	≈ ♓	♐ ♑	♐	♑ ≈	♏ ♐ ♑	≈ ♓	♐ ♑	♏ ♐	♐ ♑	♐ ♑	≈	♑ ≈	♐ ♑
date	1 3	1 18	1	1 14	1 9	1	1	1 3 28	1 24	1	1 18	1 7	1 14	1 8	1 3 27	1 23
sign	♓ ♈	≈ ♓	♐ ♑	♑ ≈	♑ ≈	≈	≈	≈ ♓ ♈	♑ ≈	♓	♓ ♈	♑ ≈	♑ ≈	≈	≈ ♓ ♈	♑ ≈
date	1 7	1 14	1 7	1 10	1 5 29	1	1 24	1 19	1 8	1 14	1 7	1 10	1 4 29	1	1 23	1 19
sign	♈ ♉	♓ ♈	≈ ♓	♈ ♉	≈ ♓ ♈	♓	♓ ♈	≈ ♓	♈ ♉	♓ ♈	♈ ♉	♓ ♈	≈ ♓ ♈	♓	♈ ♉	≈ ♓
date	1	1 8	1 2 28	1 6	1 22	1 6	1 18	1 13	1 26	1 7	1 2 27	1 6	1 22	1 7	1 17	1 12
sign	♉	♈ ♉	♈ ♓ ♈	♉ ♊	♈ ♉	≈ ♓	♉ ♊	♈ ♉	♈ ♉	♉ ♈	≈ ♓ ♈	♉ ♊	♈ ♉	≈ ♓	♉ ♊	♈ ♈
date	1 3	1 27	1 23	1 6	1 17	1 7	1 13	1 7	1	1 26	1 22	1	1 16	1 7	1 13	1 6 31
sign	♉ ♈	♉ ♊	♉ ♊	♊	♉ ♊	♓ ♈	♊	♈ ♉	♉	♉ ♈	♈ ♉	♉	♉ ♊	♓ ♈	♉ ♊	♈ ♉ ♈
date	1	1 21	1 16	1	1 10	1 4 29	1 9	1 25	1 3	1	1 20	1 16	1	1 10	1 3 29	1 24
sign	♉	♊ ♌	♉ ♊	♊	♊	♈ ♉ ♊	♊ ♋	♉ ♊	♉ ♊	♉	♊ ♌	♉ ♊	♊	♊	♈ ♉ ♊	♉ ♊
date	1 9	1 16	1 11	1	1 5 29	1 25	1	1 19	1 8	1 16	1	1 2	1 4 29	1 25	1 8	1 19
sign	♉ ♊	♊ ♋	♊ ♋	♋	♊ ♋	♊ ♋	♌	♊ ♋	♊ ♋	♋ ♌	♊	♋ ♌	♊ ♋	♊ ♋	♊ ♋	♋ ♋
date	1 6	1 11	1 5 29	1	1 23	1 19	1	1 13	1 6 31	1 11	1 4 28	1	1 22	1 19	1 20	1 12
sign	♊ ♋	♋ ♍ ♎	♊ ♋ ♌	♍ ♎	♋ ♌	♋ ♌	♍	♌ ♍	♊ ♋	♍ ♎	♋ ♌ ♌	♋	♋ ♌	♋ ♌	♋ ♋	♌ ♍
date	1 2 27	1 8	1 22	1 9	1 17	1 13	1	1 6 30	1 27	1	1 22	1 9	1 16	1 12	1	1 5 30
sign	♋ ♌ ♍	♎ ♏	♋ ♌	♋ ♌	♎ ♏	♍ ♎	♍	♍ ♎ ♏	♌ ♍	♍ ♎	♍ ♎	♋ ♌	♌ ♍	♍ ♎	♍	♍ ♎ ♏
date	1 22	1 11	1 16	1 8	1 12	1 7 31	1 25	1	1 21	1 11	1 16	1 8	1 12	1 6 30	1	1 24
sign	♍ ♎	♎ ♏	♍ ♎	♌ ♍	♍ ♎ ♏	♍ ♎ ♏	♌ ♍	♍	♎ ♏	♎ ♏	♍ ♎	♌ ♍	♍ ♎	♍ ♎ ♏	♍	♍ ♎
date	1 15	1	1 9	1 4 29	1 8	1 24	1 10	1 18	1 14	1 29	1 9	1 3 28	1 7	1 23	1 10	1 18
sign	♎ ♏	♏ ♐	♎ ♏	♎ ♏ ♐	♏	♍ ♎	♎ ♏	♏ ♐	♏ ♐	♎ ♏ ♐	♏ ♐	♎ ♏ ♏	♎ ♏	♎ ♏	♎ ♏	♏ ♐
date	1 9	1 7 31	1 3 27	1 23	1 6	1 18	1 10	1 13	1 8 31	1	1 3 27	1 22	1 6	1 18	1 9	1 13
sign	♏ ♐	♏ ♐ ♑	♏ ♐ ♑	♏ ♐	♑ ≈	♐ ♑	♏ ♐	♏ ♐ ≈	♏ ♐ ♑	♐	♏ ♐ ♑	♐ ♑	♏ ♐	♏ ♐	♎ ♏	♐ ♑

1929–1944

	1929	1930	1931	1932	1933	1934	1935	1936	1937	1938	1939	1940	1941	1942	1943	1944
date	1 7	1 24	1 4	1 20	1 15	1	1 9	1 4 28	1 7	1	1 17	1 5	1 19	1 14	1	1 9	1 4 29
sign	≈ ♓	♐ ♑	♑ ≈	≈ ♓	♐ ♑	♐	♑ ≈	♏ ♐ ♑	♐ ♓	♑ ≈	♐ ♑	♐ ♑	♐ ♑	♐ ♑	≈	♐ ♑	♐ ♑ ♑
date	1 3	1 17	1 7	1 13	1 8	1	1 2 26	1 23	1 2	1 17	1 7	1 13	1 7	1	1 2 26	1 22
sign	♓ ♈	≈ ♓	♐ ♑	♑ ≈	♑ ≈	≈	≈ ♓ ♈	♑ ≈	♓ ♈	≈ ♓	♑ ≈	♑ ≈	♑ ≈	≈	≈ ♓ ♈	♑ ≈
date	1 9	1	1 6 31	1 10	1 4 28	1	1 23	1 18	1	1 13	1 6	1 9	1 3 28	1	1 22	1 18
sign	♈ ♉	♓ ♈	♑ ≈ ♓	♈ ♉	♈ ♓ ♈	♓	♈ ♉	≈ ♓	♈ ♈	♓ ♈	♈ ♉	♓ ♈	≈ ♓ ♈	♓	♈ ♉	≈ ♓
date	1 21	1 7 30	1 27	1 5	1 21	1 7	1 17	1 12	1 15	1 6 30	1 26	1 5	1 21	1 7	1 16	1 11
sign	♉ ♈	♈ ♉ ♊	♈ ♉	♓ ♈	♉ ♊	≈ ♓	♈ ♉	♈ ♉	♉ ♈	♈ ♉ ♊	♈ ♉	♈ ♉	≈ ♓	♈ ♉	♉ ♊	♈ ♈
date	1	1	1 22	1 7	1 6	1	1 7	1 12	1 6 30	1	1 25	1 21	1 7	1	1 12	1 5 30
sign	♉	♉	♉ ♊	♊	♉ ♊	♓ ♈	♊	♈ ♉	♉ ♊	♉	♉ ♈	♉	♓ ♈	♉	♉ ♊	♈ ♉ ♈
date	1 4	1 20	1 16	1	1 9	1 3 29	1 8	1 23	1 5	1 19	1 15	1	1 9	1 3 28	1 8	1 23
sign	♈ ♉	♉ ♊	♉ ♊	♊	♊	♈ ♉ ♊	♉ ♊	♉ ♊	♈ ♉	♉ ♊	♉ ♊	♊	♊	♈ ♉ ♊	♉ ♊	♉ ♊
date	1 9	1	1	1 14 21	1 3 28	1 24	1 8	1 18	1 9	1	1 10	1 6	1 3 28	1 24	1	1 18
sign	♊ ♊	♋ ♌	♊ ♋	♊ ♋ ♍	♉ ♊ ♍	♊ ♋	♋ ♌	♊ ♋	♊ ♊	♋ ♌	♊ ♋	♋ ♊	♊ ♋	♊ ♋	♋ ♌	♊ ♋
date	1 6 31	1 11	1 4 28	1	1 22	1 18	1	1 12	1 4 31	1 10	1 3 28	1 2	1 22	1 18	1	1 11
sign	♊ ♋ ♋	♍ ♎	♊ ♋ ♌	♌ ♍	♋ ♌	♋ ♌	♍	♌ ♍	♊ ♋ ♌	♍ ♎	♋ ♌ ♌	♋ ♌	♋ ♌	♋ ♌	♋	♋ ♍
date	1 26	1 8	1 21	1 8	1 12	1 12	1	1 5 29	1 26	1 8	1 21	1 9	1 16	1	1	1 4 29
sign	♌ ♍	♎ ♏	♍ ♎	♎ ♏	♍ ♎	♋ ♌	♍	♍ ♎ ♏	♌ ♍	♍ ♎	♎ ♏	♌ ♍	♌ ♍	♍	♍ ♎ ♏	♍ ♎
date	1 21	1 13	1 15	1 8	1 12	1 6 30	1	1 24	1 20	1 14	1 15	1 7	1 11	1 6 29	1	1 23
sign	♎ ♏	♎ ♏	♍ ♎	♌ ♍	♎ ♏	♍ ♎ ♏	♌ ♍	♍	♎ ♏	♎ ♏	♍ ♎	♌ ♍	♍ ♎	♍ ♎ ♏	♍	♍ ♎
date	1 14	1	1 2 28	1 7	1 7	1	1 10	1	1 7	1 13	1	1 8	1 2 27	1 7	1 22	1 10	1 17
sign	♎ ♏	♏ ♐	♎ ♏ ♐	♎ ♏	♏ ♐	♎ ♏	♎ ♏	♏ ♐	♏ ♐	♎ ♏ ♐	♏ ♐	♎ ♏	♍ ♎ ♏	♎ ♏	♎ ♏	♎ ♏
date	1 8 31	1	1 2 26	1 22	1 5	1 17	1 9	1 12	1 7 31	1	1 2 26	1 21	1 6	1 16	1 9	1 12
sign	♏ ♐ ♑	♏	♏ ♐ ♑	♏ ♐	♐ ♑	♐ ♑	♏ ♐	♏ ♐	♏ ♐ ♑	♐	♏ ♐ ♑	♐ ♑	♏ ♐	♏ ♐	♎ ♏	♐ ♑

1945–1960

	1945	1946	1947	1948	1949	1950	1951	1952	1953	1954	1955	1956	1957	1958	1959	1960
date	1 6	1 23	1 6	1 19	1 14	1	1 8	1 3 28	1 6	1 23	1	1 7	1 18	1 13	1	1 8	1 3 28
sign	≈ ♓	♐ ♑	♑ ≈	≈ ♓	♐ ♑	≈	♑ ≈	♏ ♐ ♑	♐ ♓	♑ ≈	♐ ♑	≈ ♓	♐ ♑	♐ ♑	≈	♐ ♑	♐ ♑ ♑
date	1 3	1 16	1 7	1 11 12	1 7	1	1 25	1 22	1 3	1 16	1 7	1 11	1 6	1	1 25	1 21
sign	♓ ♈	≈ ♓	♐ ♑	♑ ≈ ≈	♑ ≈	≈	♑ ≈	♑ ≈	♓ ♈	≈ ♓	♐ ♑	♑ ≈	♑ ≈	≈	♑ ≈	♑ ≈
date	1 12	1	1 6 31	1 9	1 2 3 27	1	1 22	1 17	1 15	1 12	1 5 31	1 9	1 2 26	1	1 21	1 17
sign	♈ ♉	♓ ♈	♑ ≈ ♓	♈ ♉	♈ ♓ ♈	♓	≈ ♓	♈ ♉	♈ ♈	♓ ♈	♈ ♓ ♈	♈ ♉	♓ ♈	♓	♈ ♉	≈ ♓
date	1 8	1 6 30	1 26	1 5	1 20	1 7	1 16	1 10	1	1 5 29	1 25	1 5	1 20	1 7	1 15	1 10
sign	♉ ♈	♈ ♉ ♊	♈ ♉	♉ ♈	♉ ♊	≈ ♓	♈ ♉	♉ ♊	♉	♈ ♉ ♊	♈ ♉	♉ ♈	♈ ♉	♈ ♉	♉ ♊	♈ ♈
date	1	1 25	1	1	1	1 6	1 12	1 5 29	1	1 24	1 20	1	1 14	1 6	1 11	1 4 29
sign	♉	♉ ♈	♊ ♊	♉ ♊	♊	♓ ♈	♊	♈ ♉ ♊	♉	♉ ♈	♉	♊	♓ ♈	♉	♉ ♊	♈ ♉ ♈
date	1 6	1 19	1 14	1 30	1 9	1	1 2 28	1 8	1 23	1 6	1 18	1 14	1 24	1 7	1 2 27	1 7	1 22
sign	♈ ♉	♉ ♊	♉ ♊	♊	♊ ♋	♈ ♉ ♊	♉ ♊	♉ ♊	♈ ♉	♉ ♊	♉ ♊	♊	♊	♈ ♉ ♊	♉ ♊	♉ ♊
date	1 8	1 14	1 8 9	1	1 2 27	1	1 9	1 18	1	1 14	1 9	1	1 2 27	1 23	1 9	1 17
sign	♊ ♋	♋ ♌	♊ ♋	♊	♊ ♋	♓	♋ ♌	♊ ♋	♋	♉ ♊	♊ ♋	♊	♋ ♌	♊ ♋	♋ ♌	♊ ♋
date	1 5 30	1 10	1 3 27	1 4	1 21	1 17	1	1 5 10 31	1 5 31	1 10	1 2 26	1 5	1 21	1 17	1	1 10
sign	♊ ♋ ♋	♍ ♎	♊ ♋ ♌	♌ ♍	♋ ♌	♋ ♌	♍	♋ ♌ ♌ ♍	♊ ♋ ♌	♍ ♎	♋ ♌ ♌	♋ ♌	♋ ♌	♋ ♌	♋	♋ ♍
date	1 25	1 7	1 20	1	1 15	1 11	1	1 4 28	1 25	1 7	1 19	1	1 15	1 10	1 21 26	1 3 28
sign	♌ ♍	♎ ♏	♍ ♎	♎ ♏	♍ ♎	♋ ♌	♍	♍ ♎ ♏	♌ ♍	♍ ♎	♎ ♏	♌ ♍	♌ ♍	♍ ♎	♍ ♌ ♍	♍ ♎
date	1 20	1 17	1 14	1 7	1 11	1 5 29	1	1 23	1 19	1 24 28	1 14	1 7	1 10	1 4 28	1	1 22
sign	♎ ♏	♎ ♏	♍ ♎	♌ ♍	♎ ♏	♍ ♎ ♏	♌ ♍	♍	♎ ♏	♍ ♎ ♏	♎ ♏	♌ ♍	♍ ♎	♍ ♎ ♏	♍	♍ ♎
date	1 13	1 9	1 7	1 2 27	1 27	1 22	1 10	1 16	1	1 12	1 7 30	1 26	1 6	1 21	1 10	1 16
sign	♎ ♏	♏ ♏	♎ ♏	♎ ♏	♏ ♐	♎ ♏	♎ ♏	♎ ♏	♏ ♐	♎ ♏	♎ ♏ ♏	♎ ♏	♎ ♏	♏ ♐	♎ ♏	♎ ♏
date	1 7 31	1	1 25	1 21	1 7	1 15	1 9	1 11	1 6 30	1	1 25	1 20	1 7	1 15	1 9	1 11
sign	♏ ♐ ♑	♏	♏ ♐	♏ ♐	♐ ♑	♐ ♑	♏ ♐	♐ ♑	♏ ♐ ♑	♐	♏ ♐	♐ ♑	♏ ♐	♐ ♑	♐ ♑	≈ ♑

Index